photographing
Baltimore, Annapolis
& Maryland's Eastern Shore
Where to Find Perfect Shots and How to Take Them

David Muse

D1296617

THE COUNTRYMAN PRESS
WOODSTOCK, VERMONT

This book is dedicated to my wife, Kitty, for her endless patience and encouragement. LYTIAB!

Maps by Paul Woodward, © The Countryman Press
Book design and composition by S. E. Livingston

Photographing Baltimore, Annapolis
& Maryland's Eastern Shore
978-0-88150-960-1

Published by The Countryman Press,
P.O. Box 748, Woodstock, VT 05091

Distributed by W. W. Norton & Company, Inc.,
500 Fifth Avenue, New York, NY 10110

Printed in the United States of America

10 9 8 7 6 5 4 3 2 1

Title Page: Colorful fishing buoys await another day of service out on Chesapeake Bay.
Right: A family on their way to visit the Power Plant

Acknowledgments

Special thanks go to:

David Middleton, Rod Barbee, and Jeff Wendorff for their years of friendship and professional support

The crew at Countryman Press, including Kermit Hummel, Lisa Sacks, and Barbara Jatkola, for making this project an exciting adventure

Maryland photographer Middleton Evans for his birding site suggestions

David Luria, director of Washington Photo Safari, for his guidance and assistance

And to my students, whose curiosity and drive inspire me.

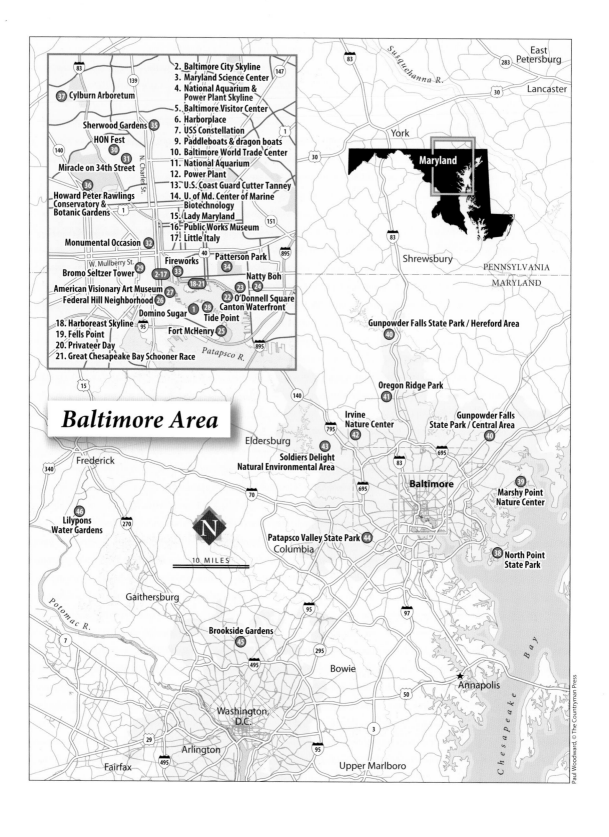

Baltimore Area

Cylburn Arboretum 37
Sherwood Gardens 35
HON Fest 30
31
Miracle on 34th Street
Howard Peter Rawlings
Conservatory &
Botanic Gardens 36
Monumental Occasion 32
W. Mullberry St.
Fireworks
Bromo Seltzer Tower 29
2-17 33
18-21
American Visionary Art Museum 27
Federal Hill Neighborhood 26
Domino Sugar 1
28
Tide Point
Fort McHenry 25

18. Harboreast Skyline
19. Fells Point
20. Privateer Day
21. Great Chesapeake Bay Schooner Race

2. Baltimore City Skyline
3. Maryland Science Center
4. National Aquarium &
   Power Plant Skyline
5. Baltimore Visitor Center
6. Harborplace
7. USS Constellation
9. Paddleboats & dragon boats
10. Baltimore World Trade Center
11. National Aquarium
12. Power Plant
13. U.S. Coast Guard Cutter Tanney
14. U. of Md. Center of Marine
    Biotechnology
15. Lady Maryland
16. Public Works Museum
17. Little Italy

Patterson Park
34
Natty Boh
23 24
22 O'Donnell Square
Canton Waterfront

Maryland

East
Petersburg
Lancaster
York
Shrewsbury
PENNSYLVANIA
MARYLAND

Gunpowder Falls State Park / Hereford Area 40

Oregon Ridge Park 41

Irvine
Nature Center 42
Eldersburg
Soldiers Delight
Natural Environmental Area 43

Gunpowder Falls
State Park / Central Area 40

Baltimore

Marshy Point
Nature Center 39

North Point
State Park 38

Frederick

Lilypons
Water Gardens 46

N
10 MILES

Patapsco Valley State Park 44
Columbia

Gaithersburg

Brookside Gardens 45

Bowie

Annapolis

Washington,
D.C.

Arlington

Fairfax

Upper Marlboro

Chesapeake Bay

Susquehanna R.
Potomac R.
Patapsco R.

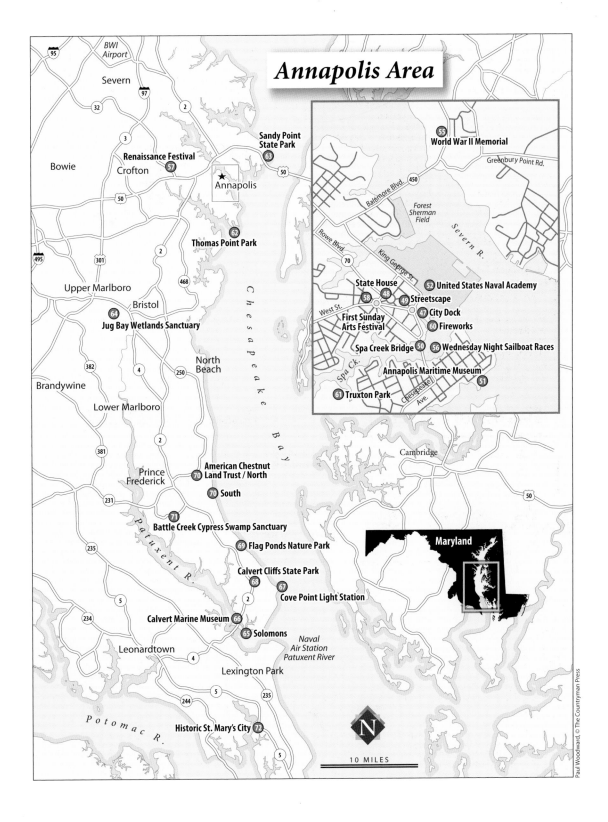

Annapolis Area

55 World War II Memorial

Greenbury Point Rd.

Baltimore Blvd.

450

Forest Sherman Field

Rowe Blvd.

King George St.

70

Severn R.

52 United States Naval Academy

State House

58 48 49 Streetscape

West St.

First Sunday Arts Festival

47 City Dock

60 Fireworks

Spa Creek Bridge 50

56 Wednesday Night Sailboat Races

Spa Ck.

Annapolis Maritime Museum

Chesapeake Ave.

51

61 Truxton Park

BWI Airport

95

Severn

97

32

3

Bowie

Crofton

Renaissance Festival 57

50

Annapolis

Sandy Point State Park 63

50

62 Thomas Point Park

2

Upper Marlboro

495

301

468

Bristol

64 Jug Bay Wetlands Sanctuary

North Beach

382

4

250

Brandywine

Lower Marlboro

2

381

231

Prince Frederick

American Chestnut Land Trust / North 70

70 South

71 Battle Creek Cypress Swamp Sanctuary

235

69 Flag Ponds Nature Park

Calvert Cliffs State Park

68

67 Cove Point Light Station

5

234

Calvert Marine Museum 66

65 Solomons

Naval Air Station Patuxent River

Leonardtown

4

Lexington Park

244

235

5

Historic St. Mary's City 72

Potomac R.

5

Patuxent R.

Chesapeake Bay

Cambridge

50

Maryland

N

10 MILES

Paul Woodward, © The Countryman Press

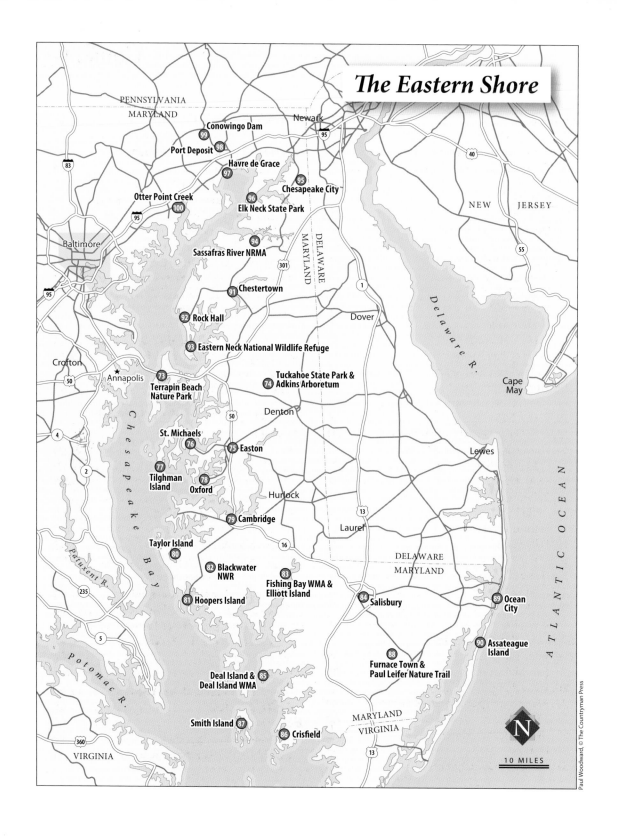

The Eastern Shore

PENNSYLVANIA
MARYLAND

Newark

99 Conowingo Dam

Port Deposit **98**

97 Havre de Grace

95 Chesapeake City

Otter Point Creek **100**

96 Elk Neck State Park

NEW JERSEY

Baltimore

DELAWARE
MARYLAND

94 Sassafras River NRMA

91 Chestertown

Dover

92 Rock Hall

Delaware R.

93 Eastern Neck National Wildlife Refuge

Crofton

Cape May

Annapolis

73 Tuckahoe State Park &
74 Adkins Arboretum

Terrapin Beach
Nature Park

Denton

St. Michaels
76

75 Easton

Lewes

77 Tilghman
Island

78
Oxford

Hurlock

79 Cambridge

Laurel

Taylor Island
80

82 Blackwater
NWR

83

DELAWARE
MARYLAND

Fishing Bay WMA &
Elliott Island

81 Hoopers Island

84 Salisbury

89 Ocean
City

ATLANTIC OCEAN

90 Assateague
Island

88

Furnace Town &
Paul Leifer Nature Trail

Deal Island &
Deal Island WMA **85**

MARYLAND
VIRGINIA

Smith Island **87**

86 Crisfield

VIRGINIA

Chesapeake Bay

Patuxent R.

Potomac R.

N

10 MILES

Paul Woodward, © The Countryman Press

Contents

Maryland's quintessential seafood dish

Introduction

My wife and I grew up in the Midwest, lived in Germany for a number of years, and moved to Baltimore some 30 years ago. We raised our daughters here and now have only a few blocks to walk to visit our granddaughter. We consider Baltimore and Maryland our home.

While Maryland ranks just 42nd in size among the 50 states, it's bursting at the seams with a tremendous variety of nature, travel, and urban sights to explore and photograph. You can choose a dazzling seashore; distinct physiographic areas (coastal plain, Piedmont region, ridges and valleys, Appalachian plateau); the Chesapeake Bay, the country's largest estuary; picturesque harbors and marinas; mountains and colorful fall foliage; charming and captivating cities, towns, and villages; and much more.

Okay, I have to admit that Maryland does not have a desert, but we do have a wild side, complete with native cactus and rattlesnakes. You will find the eastern prickly pear cactus along the Bay, but all the rattlesnakes are in our western mountains (phew!).

This book is a result of my explorations and the photo workshops I teach. It provides equal coverage of urban sights, natural spots, and photogenic seasonal events. I have included my favorite places and events in Baltimore, Annapolis, and around Maryland's Eastern Shore. Whether you are a Maryland resident looking to discover more of what our state has to offer, a visitor hoping to capture some great shots during your travels, or a seasoned photographer seeking to expand your portfolio, this guide tells you where to find the best shots and how to create them.

The sights I recommend consistently provide top-notch photo opportunities. Given the cornucopia of wonderful sights around Bal-

Awaiting the Great Chesapeake Bay Schooner Race in Baltimore

timore, Annapolis, and Maryland's Eastern Shore, I may have missed one or two of your favorite sites. If so, send me an e-mail via my Web site, www.davidmusephoto.com, and I will see about including them in the next edition.

For detailed information on lodging, museums, restaurants, shops, and other places of interest, I suggest that you buy a copy of Allison Blake's Explorer's Guide *Baltimore, Annapolis & the Chesapeake Bay: A Great Destination* (Countryman Press, 2010). Then pack your camera gear, program your car's GPS, and begin your photo safari through Baltimore, Annapolis, and Maryland's Eastern Shore.

Best wishes . . . and see you on the road.

The Lady Maryland *is a replica of a 19th-century pungy schooner.*

How to Use This Book

Where, when, and how is what this book is all about. My goal here is the same as that of the photo workshops I teach: to guide you to key photogenic sites in the Baltimore, Annapolis, and Eastern Shore region during the best times to visit, and to help you, once there, create the best images.

I have divided this guide into three parts and begin descriptions from a central site in each part, but you can start your photo tour from anywhere around the Eastern Shore. The descriptions give you the flexibility to plan everything from an "I have a few hours to shoot" outing to a much longer photography-packed trip.

I describe the possible photo opportunities you will find at each place and event. While these descriptions vary in length and detail, each site is intriguing and well worth the time to visit.

I recommend what to do, as well as some things not to do. In particular, do not trespass on private property, or you may get a *shot* you were not expecting. At the end of many descriptions, I include a Web site to assist you in finding additional details. Where appropriate, I include a specific tip to help you enhance particular photos.

The lens recommendations I make are usually of a general nature, such as wide-angle or moderate telephoto. You can capture and create wonderful images with any camera, but note that any specific lens recommendations I list are in 35mm equivalents.

In the next section, I explain a number of general thoughts, techniques, recommendations, and ideas on how best to capture and enhance your images. These include a few oft-repeated tips, such as use a tripod and cable/remote release for sharp images, along with some things you may not have heard before, such as look *first* for good background and get down to the level of your subject (dirty knees are a sign of a good photographer). Before I proceed, here is one tip most outdoor and travel photography instructors fail to mention: Buy a good pair of hiking or walking shoes, preferably waterproof. Believe me, you will thank me later for that recommendation.

Use this book as a guide, and you will capture a number of images guaranteed to knock the visual socks off your family and friends. There is a vast wealth of photo opportunities around Baltimore, Annapolis, and Maryland's Eastern Shore. I strongly encourage you to explore this area on your own, too.

Commercial fishing boats in Ocean City harbor

How I Photograph Baltimore, Annapolis, and Maryland's Eastern Shore

Storytelling

I believe storytelling is of such critical importance that I highlight it here before I talk about where to find great images and how to create them. Storytelling is a simple technique guaranteed to wow your viewer. Many photographers show viewers all the images they shot on a trip, often in the order they created them.

Break that mold! Captivate your viewer by telling a series of visual stories. For example, use your best five or six images of a commercial harbor, historic skipjacks and other workboats, piles of crab pots, or bushel baskets of blue crabs and Bay oysters to illustrate the life of a Chesapeake waterman.

It's Your Image

I use the aperture priority shooting mode to create the vast majority of my images; the manual mode 5–10 percent of the time; and the shutter priority mode for the occasional action shot. I strongly encourage you to select a shooting mode other than automatic. When set to fully automatic, your camera makes all the decisions about exposure, depth of field, and action. In essence, it takes the picture. Since you are serious about photography (you bought this book, right?), you will get more pleasing results by taking more control of the process. Use techniques and hone skills that will help you create images that satisfy your artistic drive. If you are satisfied, it's a success. It's your image.

Look around First

I generally have a specific subject in mind when I head out to photograph. I try not to rush things; rather, I keep my eyes and ears open for the unexpected. I find I get better results when I first invest time and energy looking around for the best subject, angle of view, and lighting conditions. This method applies equally to cityscapes, landscapes, and nature and event photography.

Let's examine this "look around first" process. Keep in mind that your camera is still

Crabs fresh off a Chesapeake waterman's boat

in your bag. You want a photo that shows you spent a day or two in Baltimore and found it an attractive place to visit. You see the sign at the visitor center and realize that it will clearly inform your viewer that you were in Baltimore. You begin to look around and evaluate possible compositions. You decide that your initial view (above left) does not work because there is too much sky, the lamppost is intrusive, and the cruise ship looks like an afterthought. You then ask yourself, What about a vertical composition? You see that certainly does not work any better (above right), so you check options available from the opposite side of the visitor center sign. Hey, you say to yourself, that looks way better. My viewer can see that Baltimore is busy with people. Do you get out your camera now? Nope! You see that the light is dull and decide to check back on conditions later (right). That afternoon the blue sky and sidelight are several times more attractive than before. Now you take out your camera and create the shot (opposite).

Should you return after dinner, you might shout *Holy crabs!* to yourself (Marylanders love crabs—the seafood variety, not the old curmudgeons). Evening twilight provides fantastic light, so you shoot the sign and skyline

BALTIMORE VISITOR CENTER

A container ship passes the confluence of the Bay and the Patuxent River.

again (left). By first taking time to look around and evaluate the light and conditions, you captured two great images versus several dull ones. The practice of taking time to find a good subject in the right light and composing the shot carefully pays big dividends.

It's All about the Light

Photography is all about capturing light in a pleasing way. We photograph the light on a particular subject rather than the subject itself. Shoot a good subject in dull light, and your image will be dull. Photograph a good subject in great light, and your image will be fantastic. Here are my recommendations for various lighting conditions.

Predawn and Evening Twilight

If you want incredible light, arrive before sunrise and stay out after sunset. Often the sky seems to glow in photographs shot during these times. The best light happens quickly, so you have to be in place with your tripod set in position. Landscapes look great in twilight, and twilit skylines and cityscapes can be stunning.

Once evening twilight fades, you can often continue to shoot cityscapes for 5–10 minutes by changing your white balance to tungsten. Should your camera not offer that setting, adjust the white balance afterward using postprocessing software. For such images, apply minimal saturation and vibrance adjustments to avoid an unnatural appearance.

A gigantic cloud over the Fishing Bay Wildlife Management Area

Sunrise and Sunset

For good reason, photographers describe the hour after sunrise and before sunset as "magic." The low angle of the sun produces beautiful warm colors, and the level of shadowing enhances the dimensionality of your images. This light is ideal for nature, travel, and urban photography. Use of crosslighting at these times can produce phenomenal results.

Clear Blue Sky

On a clear-blue-sky morning or afternoon, head to City Dock in Annapolis, to Baltimore's Inner Harbor, or to any of the commercial harbors around the Bay. There you can capture mirrorlike reflections of the skyline when the waters are calm. Generally, puffy white clouds and a clear blue sky add a sparkle to pastoral landscapes, coastal views, and cityscapes. Water surfaces will have a bluer hue than the sky, so marinas and fishing vessels will appear brighter. Look for reflections on water, car hoods, and windows, because they will extend your shooting time.

Rain and Overcast Sky

When it's pouring rain, visit and photograph an indoor market or maritime museum. However, when there is a light mist or overcast sky, make your way to a county park, state park, or nature center. Wildflowers and forest scenes look better under these conditions. Reflections on wet city streets provide a different perspective and view otherwise not available.

Fog

If there is fog, do not pass Go! Head straight for the nearest harbor or marina, where fog generally will lend a wow-inducing ethereal feel to your images. Remember to use your exposure-compensation function. Add 1/3 to 2/3 of a stop so the fog looks light and bright versus dull and drab.

Clear + Concise = Appealing Composition

When your image clearly conveys your vision, it is effective. When your image confuses the viewer, it is ineffective. What to do? Ask yourself what you like about the scene. Then exclude anything that detracts from the main subject. Often getting closer, either physically or via a zoom lens, enhances a composition. I arrange the parts of my image so they contribute to a visual story. The clearer and more concise you make your composition, the wider its appeal will be.

I use the same techniques to shoot natural landscapes and cityscapes. I look for foreground elements that help direct the viewer's attention into the image and accentuate the main subject. Without a foreground element, skylines and their watery reflections (particularly those images shot at a 90-degree angle) often appear as a flat facade regardless of the aperture selected. In Baltimore and around the Chesapeake Bay, there is a simple solution: Wait for a boat. As it sails by, it adds a sense of three-dimensionality to an otherwise flat image.

A night heron seeks its supper from a dockside vantage point.

Background

No matter what I am photographing, once I find an interesting subject in good light I evaluate the background and decide how to deal with any distracting elements. If I cannot eliminate background distractions by changing position or minimize their effect by using a narrower depth of field to blur them, I look for a different subject. That's right. I will not photograph a good subject in good light if the background will distract from the appeal and effectiveness of my image.

Background is so important that one technique I recommend for travel and urban photography is to first find a good background setting and then wait for someone or something interesting to enter the picture: a person wearing colorful clothing, a cyclist in a crowd of pedestrians, an individual carrying an umbrella on a sunny day, and so on.

Conditions

After I evaluate the light, my subject, and its background, I check everything else before I click the shutter release. Shooting workboats and Chesapeake watermen in a harbor? Be sure there is little or no flotsam in the water. Photographing spring wildflowers in a state park? Verify there is no breeze to make the flowers sway. If existing conditions adversely affect the quality of your image, move to a different subject, choose to shoot another day, or adjust your image.

Obviously, weather is one condition you need to consider. Whether the weather is hot or cold, wet or dry, if you are comfortable and

Sometimes the someone who enters the picture is very interesting! The higher the hair, the closer to heaven—Baltimore's annual Honfest (see page 43).

ready to work, your camera will be ready, willing, and able. Keep a spare battery handy in a pocket, and carry a plastic bag (or a store-bought rain cover) to help keep rain and snow off your gear.

Equipment

Tripod

Camera movement causes an image to lose sharp focus. Use of a sturdy tripod and a cable/remote release eliminates camera movement. For example, without a tripod it would be impossible to use the long exposures required for twilight and wildflower photos. More important, a tripod forces the photographer to devote proper time to evaluating and organizing clear and concise compositions. I consider a tripod essential camera gear and use one for all my nature, travel, and urban photography. For event photography, I often hand hold the camera and use a higher ISO setting. Buy the best tripod you can afford. Look for one that reaches your eye level or higher when fully extended. This will spare you neck pain. Ideally, your tripod should also allow you to get close to the ground.

Polarizing Filter and UV Filter

Another must-have piece of equipment is a circular polarizer. It filters out glare, haze, and reflections. A polarizer helps to darken a too-bright sky; cuts glare on flowers, foliage, glass, and water; and enhances color overall. After attaching it to the lens, rotate the filter until you achieve a pleasing effect. Polarization is strongest when the sun is to your right or left and weakest when the sun is directly in front of or behind you.

Remove and stow any filter until circumstances call for its use. A lot of folks keep a skylight/UV filter on their cameras. The lens cap included with your camera, plus a lens hood, provide far more protection for your lens than a skylight/UV filter can deliver. Moreover, I feel strongly that only two circumstances call for a UV filter: first, to protect against blowing sand while on a beach or in the desert; second, instead of a polarizer at altitudes above 3,000 feet to produce more natural-looking skies.

Neutral-Density Filters

The human eye can see a wider range of light than a camera can "see" and accurately record. A graduated neutral-density (grad ND) filter is a blessing when you encounter a scene whose foreground and background are out of balance, such as a cityscape or landscape with a bright sky. One half of the grad ND filter is dark, the other completely clear. The graduated dark half reduces the difference in brightness of your scene so that you can record detail in both the shadow and highlight areas. Grad ND filters come in different strengths. Generally, they reduce the brightness by one, two, or three stops of light. To determine what strength filter to use, take two meter readings: one with the darker portion of the scene filling the whole frame and one with the sky filling the frame. Place the appropriate grad ND filter in front of your lens, use the depth of field preview button to position it properly, and then rely on your matrix or evaluative meter to compute a properly balanced exposure. Check your histogram and make any necessary adjustments.

I use a split neutral-density filter with a hard transition between the dark and light halves when shooting scenes with a distinct linear break—for example, between water and sky in a Chesapeake Bay sunrise scene.

Lens Hood

The final item I consider essential camera gear is a lens hood. It prevents stray light from leaking in from the sides of your front lens element, thereby reducing lens flare and enhancing contrast. Use a lens hood and you will find that your images have more saturated color.

Event Photography

Marylanders celebrate a smorgasbord of fairs, festivals, historic reenactments, parades, and other events each year. Several are outrageously funny, some are a real hoot, and a few are merely hilarious. But all are interesting and a blast to photograph. For these events, I generally carry only my 28–70mm lens and its lens hood; use aperture priority, matrix (evaluative) metering; and dial in a minus 0.3 exposure compensation to ward off unexpected background highlights. I pack an extra battery and several memory cards in my pocket. On sunny days, I also bring my flash unit to balance out facial shadows. You have to get close to your subject, so I always ask the person if I may photograph him or her. I do not bother with a model release since I do not intend to license such images for other than editorial use.

General Cautions

You will be photographing on waterfront promenades and piers, in commercial fishing harbors and marinas filled with sailboats, on narrow streets in riverside towns, and all along the Chesapeake Bay shoreline. Watch your step. You do not want to take a plunge into the water. Watch your photo gear. You do not want to send any of it into the briny deep.

In several locations, you may encounter a copperhead, one of Maryland's venomous snakes. Generally, if you leave snakes alone, they will leave you alone. For the most part, people are bitten while trying to handle or kill a snake. Do not take any chances. Avoid these snakes. Note that Maryland law prohibits killing any snake, so do not risk a bite from the law either.

In Maryland parks and nature preserves, you may see four native orchids: crane-fly orchid, pink lady's slipper, rattlesnake plantain, and showy orchis. Take care not to disturb the extremely delicate microclimates of these orchids.

Beware of sand and salt water. Sand particles can get inside a camera and damage the lens mount and image sensor. Change lenses indoors, not on the beach. Sand particles and saltwater crystals can ruin tripod segment joints. When using a tripod on the beach, extend the legs far enough to keep sand and water away from all segment joints. Rinse the lower tripod legs thoroughly in fresh water to remove any sand particles and saltwater residue.

Summary

To paraphrase the old proverb about silk purses and pigs' ears, you can't make a great image out of a mediocre capture. Until someone invents King Midas image-processing software that magically turns a so-so capture into a golden image with one click of the mouse, the best option for producing a great image is to get it right in the camera.

Take time to find a good subject. Evaluate the light, background, and existing conditions. Use a tripod and cable/remote release to both steady your camera and help fashion a clear, concise composition. Exercise control over your camera rather than letting it make automatic choices. Check your histogram and make the necessary exposure-compensation adjustments. Delete any and all images you feel are unsuccessful. Use image-processing software to maximize your good images. Shoot on a regular basis, and you will become a *click* thinker—that is, the operation of your camera will be intuitive.

Baltimore, Annapolis, and Maryland's Eastern Shore have tremendous photogenic sights in store. Turn the page to see where to find them. Remember always to let your imagination and creativity serve as additional guides.

Passengers aboard the original Dove *founded Maryland's first English colony in 1634.*

A winter's eve in the Inner Harbor

I. Baltimore

Famous for its crabcakes, the Inner Harbor, Edgar Allan Poe, gritty TV cop shows, John Waters and *Hairspray,* Fort McHenry and "The Star-Spangled Banner," and the Orioles and Ravens, Baltimore draws more than 11 million tourists annually. A working harbor, cityscapes, historic sites, boats of all shapes and sizes, festivals and fireworks, and nature and the great outdoors are a few of the photographic subjects the greater Baltimore area offers.

The Inner Harbor

Navigating your visit to the Inner Harbor is easy. A pedestrian promenade circles the Inner Harbor and then winds along the waterfront through several historic neighborhoods, a distance of nearly 8 miles. Photo opportunities along this promenade will keep you busy for several days and evenings. My description of what to shoot starts with Baltimore's iconic Domino Sugar refinery and its neon sign, but you can start your photo tour of the Inner Harbor anywhere along the waterfront promenade.

Two quick notes before we begin:

• I have not included every popular tourist site and special event you could visit in Baltimore because many provide good snapshots rather than great travel images.

• Street parking near the Inner Harbor is limited to four hours. Street parking in the surrounding neighborhoods is by permit only, but nonresidents may park for free for up to two hours during certain times. Pay close attention to posted parking restrictions, especially those in effect on weekends and during stadium events. Parking is regularly enforced, so do not risk an expensive parking ticket. Use one of the parking lots and garages surrounding the Inner Harbor and in the nearby neighborhoods.

Okay, grab your camera gear, and let's get started.

The **Domino Sugar sign (1)** is a huge neon light that shimmers and shines across the Inner Harbor and over the rooftops of the surrounding neighborhoods. Predawn, first light, and evening twilight are ideal to photograph the sign. Position yourself near the HarborView tower, accessible via the intersection of Pier-

side Drive and Key Highway. Include the marina as foreground in your composition, or walk west along the promenade to photograph the refinery and sign alone across the open waters of the harbor. During the summer months, position yourself to catch the sun rising behind the sugar refinery. During late summer and early fall, position yourself to catch the full moon rising behind the refinery. Most winters, part of the harbor freezes, so take advantage of the Domino sign casting its reflection across the ice. A lens in the 28–70mm range will serve you well for most compositions. Use a telephoto lens to zoom in for detailed shots of the

The Domino Sugar refinery on a cold night

The first light of day bathes the Maryland Science Center.

refinery smokestacks, the container ships and cranes, reflections, and so on.

Pro tip: Along this stretch of the promenade, a graduated neutral-density (grad ND) filter often proves beneficial.

Continue clockwise (west) along the promenade. The stretch between the Rusty Scupper restaurant and the Maryland Science Center provides sweeping views of the **Baltimore skyline (2)** across the harbor. East of the Rusty Scupper, the skyline often looks radiant in predawn light. For evening twilight photos, you can include the Rusty Scupper and its reflection in wide-angle compositions of the city skyline. Take care to avoid glare from the bright lights along the promenade's edge. West of the Rusty Scupper, the marina and its reflection provide excellent foreground elements for skyline compositions. Here use a narrow aperture of f/16 or f/22 to keep the reflection, boats, and skyline in sharp focus.

The **Maryland Science Center (3)** is a great place for families to visit. Inside you can create family portraits and travel snapshots of dinosaurs and other exhibits. Reserve serious photography efforts for capturing early morning and evening twilight views of the building and its reflection from the sight-seeing tour boat pier, located a few hundred feet farther

A water taxi glides through the Inner Harbor on a summer afternoon.

along the promenade. In the early morning, you can capture distinctive images of the skyline reflected in the Science Center windows. In the late afternoon, the arriving water taxis are in good light. Use an aperture that will slightly blur the skyline behind the water taxis, say f/4 or f/5.6.

As you proceed past the Science Center, you will see the **National Aquarium and Power Plant skyline (4)** to the east across the water. This is a must-have photo, but daytime images of these buildings often appear as a flat facade, even when there is a good reflection in the water. If this is the case during your visit, simply wait for a passing boat (such as a water taxi) to cross in front of the National Aquarium to give your image the needed depth and dimension. When the Inner Harbor freezes during the winter, intriguing lines and patterns appear in the ice and provide good foreground for these skyline images.

Stop at the **Baltimore Visitor Center (5)** for information on activities in town and to buy water taxi tickets. The building and its grounds provide impressive late afternoon and evening twilight images. A wide-angle lens in the 24mm range is the ideal choice. Ships from around the world visit Baltimore and generally dock near the Visitor Center. You may see historic tall ships, naval warships, or other seagoing vessels. Generally, the best views are from the harbor sight-seeing boat pier, from Harborplace, and from Constellation Pier. Check www.sail baltimore.org for the arriving ships schedule.

Not only is **Harborplace (6)** my preferred spot to photograph water taxis, but most days from late spring through early fall you can find artists, musicians, and street performers here.

It's enormous fun to relax, watch, and capture the entertainment. Use your wide-angle lens to create images that include the colorful Harborplace banner, the activity, and the crowd. Use your telephoto lens to capture portraits of the individual performers and candid shots of the spectators. A wide aperture softly blurs the background of these images.

The historic **USS *Constellation* (7)** is docked at Harborplace. This is the U.S. Navy's last all-sail warship. Built in 1854, it is now a floating museum. Photographing the USS *Constellation* is challenging. Eliminating the distracting background from wide-angle shots is difficult, and controlling light contrast in compositions shot facing the stem or stern is tricky. Look for interesting patterns in its masts and rigging, in particular on clear-blue-sky days, or do a tight shot of the nameplate across its stern. I personally prefer to shoot the USS *Constellation* at dawn or dusk. Fog helps to create images that evoke impressions of the *Constellation*'s bygone era. Winter images are simply fun. Before you visit Baltimore, check www.historicships.org for upcoming events. The USS *Constellation* conducts an annual turnaround cruise each year to minimize damage to its hull. Good locations from which to photograph her under way are from the promenade near the Rusty Scupper restaurant, from behind the National Aquarium, and from the Tide Point boardwalk.

The ***Pride of Baltimore II* (8)** is a replica of an early 19th-century schooner. Not only is this tall ship a majestic symbol of the maritime history of the Chesapeake Bay, but it travels around the seven seas as Maryland's goodwill ambassador. Check www.pride2.org to see when it will be in port. Good vantage points from which to photograph the *Pride of Baltimore II* as it returns home are Fort McHenry, Tide Point, Canton Waterfront Park, Broadway Pier in Fells Point, and the waterfront promenade. It docks at several locations in the Inner Harbor, which will allow you to get detailed shots of its rigging, nameplate, and so on. At the end of its sailing season in early November, a Baltimore Fire Department boat often greets it with a gigantic salute from its water cannons. You can use both wide-angle and

The Pride of Baltimore II, *a replica of an 1812-era schooner, sails into home port.*

telephoto lenses to good advantage photographing this ship under sail and in port.

Be sure to shoot images of the **paddleboats and dragon boats (9)** next to Constellation Pier. They are a critical element in predawn compositions of the National Aquarium skyline. On clear-blue-sky days, have fun creating abstract images of their colorful reflections.

A vertiginous view of Baltimore's World Trade Center

Capture great shots of the **World Trade Center (10)**, designed by famed architect I. M. Pei, from along the South Shore and West Shore Promenade and reflected in the windows of the various buildings surrounding the Inner Harbor. From the observation deck on the 27th floor, you have a panoramic view of the harbor and surrounding neighborhoods, but conditions generally hamper quality photography from up top.

Due east of the World Trade Center is the **National Aquarium (11)**, Baltimore's preeminent tourist destination. The aquarium features hundreds of exhibits that bring you face-to-fin with the critters. The aquarium is a tremendous place to visit. Since tripods are prohibited and interior light levels are low, reserve serious photography efforts for capturing the building's exterior. Its architecture is a striking mix of pyramids and other geometric shapes, patterns, colors, and glass, all reaching toward the sky. Dawn, late afternoon, and evening twilight provide the best light for photography. Throughout the day, shoot details of the lightship *Chesapeake* and the submarine USS *Torsk* docked alongside the aquarium. Behind the aquarium buildings, capture images of passing boats, people enjoying the harbor views, and the Domino Sugar refinery across the water.

In days gone by, the **Power Plant (12)** generated electricity for city streetcars. Today the complex houses the Hard Rock Cafe, a major bookstore, and several restaurants. The old smokestacks and the 68-foot-tall neon Hard Rock guitar tower over the plaza. Use a wide-angle lens to photograph the complex from ground level. Search the windows of the National Aquarium and the surrounding office buildings for fun-house-mirror reflections of the Power Plant. The Gay Street pedestrian overpass offers a panoramic view of the plaza. You can photograph here throughout the day.

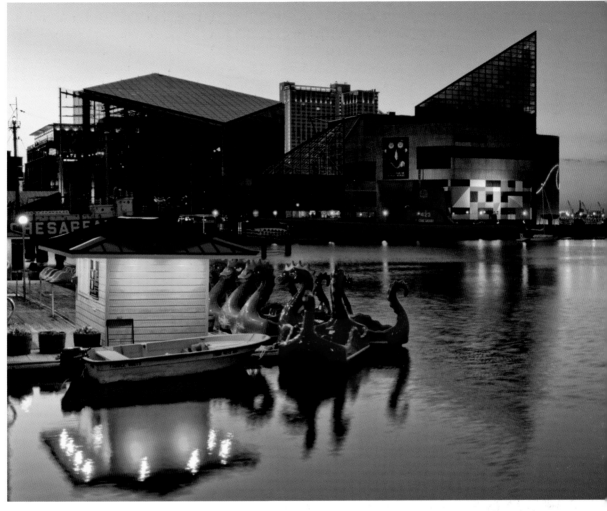

The National Aquarium and the dragon boats await a new day and new visitors.

Dawn and dusk provide the most impressive light.

Proceed around the Power Plant and cross the pedestrian footbridge. Turn around and look up for a view many photographers fail to find. The sidelight on the smokestacks and the Hard Rock Cafe guitar makes them stand in stark contrast to the twilight sky.

Behind the Power Plant are two interesting photo opportunities. The historic **U.S. Coast Guard cutter *Taney* (13)** became part of the Baltimore Maritime Museum fleet in the late 1980s. Evening twilight is the ideal time to photograph it from along Pratt Street. Adjacent to the *Taney* is the **University of Maryland Center of Marine Biotechnology (14)**. During evening twilight, its tentlike canopies provide a whimsical subject. They have an otherworldly appearance if you let your imagination run wild. Has a spacecraft from a 1950s-era science fiction movie landed in Baltimore? A telephoto lens works to good effect here.

Roof canopies at the University of Maryland Center of Marine Biotechnology at twilight

light, the Domino Sugar sign supplies an interesting backdrop.

Proceed past Pier 5 to the **Baltimore Public Works Museum (16)**. Often its cupolas, copper roof, and smokestack glow in the golden light of late afternoon. The building provides excellent contrast whenever dramatic skies appear behind it.

Take a delightful detour through **Little Italy (17)**. Widely known as one of Baltimore's culinary hot spots, it is a captivating and picturesque neighborhood dating back to the late 19th century. Start in Columbus Square and photograph the famous voyager atop his pedestal. Stroll through the narrow streets in the late afternoon and early evening. Symbols of the old country abound; even the fire hydrants are painted green, white, and red like the Italian flag. Colorful murals grace many walls. In the warm months, you may capture images of a spirited game of bocce. Use evening twilight to create colorful streetscapes featuring the many neon signs of the community's fine restaurants.

South of Little Italy on the corner of Lancaster and Caroline streets is an intriguing evening twilight view of the new **Harbor East skyline (18)** reflected in the street-side canal. You can capture a different and equally wonderful view of the Harbor East skyline from the waterfront promenade near the Rusty Scupper restaurant. A wide-angle lens equivalent to 24mm and a grad ND filter are your best choices.

Proceed along the water to the Pier 5 promenade. From late spring through early fall, historic ships such as the schooners **Lady Maryland (15)** and *Sultana* (out of Chestertown) dock here. Throughout the day, you can capture detailed images of their sails and rigging, their nameplates, and reflections in the water. During late afternoon and evening twi-

Proceed south on Caroline Street to Thames Street (rhymes with *James,* as opposed to London's famed river) and turn left. You are now in Baltimore's historic **Fells Point (19)** neighborhood. During colonial times, Fells Point was famous for shipbuilding and shipping. During the War of 1812, it was infamous for the privateers who harassed British ships. Nowadays its many fine pubs, restaurants,

The Public Works Museum glows in the last light of day.

The new Harbor East skyline from Fells Point

Colorful signs in historic Fells Point

unique shops, and annual events attract locals and tourists alike. Fells Point can keep a photographer busy from dawn to dusk. Chester Cove, Crescent Point, and Henderson's Wharf offer images of sailboats and harbor lights shimmering on the water under the radiant predawn sky. Shoot the sun rising over the marinas. First light and early light on the Domino Sugar refinery and the nearby container ships can be dramatic and dazzling. Check early morning reflections of Thames Street in the harbor waters. From Broadway Pier shoot such early morning boat activity as the water taxis gearing up for the day and tugboats streaming by. Shop windows, pub signs, historic homes, architectural details, and colorful local residents will keep you busy from morning to afternoon. From the south end of Ann Street, Broadway Pier, Bond Street Wharf,

and the Frederick Douglass–Isaac Myers Maritime Park you have excellent evening twilight views of the Domino Sugar refinery, container ships, industrial park, and Tide Point complex sparkling across the river.

Ahoy, matey! Thar's many a pirate and a buxom wench to photograph on **Privateer Day (20)** in April. Fantastic costumes, colorful characters, and historic ships invade the Fells Point waterfront near Broadway Pier. Generally, all you need to cover this event is a wide-angle lens in the range of 28–70mm and an aperture of f/5.6.

In mid-October the **Great Chesapeake Bay Schooner Race (21)** begins in Fells Point and ends down the Bay in Portsmouth, Virginia. A fleet of more than 40 schooners has participated in recent years. Among them were the *Pride of Baltimore II;* the *Mystic Whaler* from

The Great Chesapeake Bay Schooner Race in Baltimore harbor

New London, Connecticut; the *Arabella* from Newport, Rhode Island; and New Jersey's tall ship the *A. J. Meerwald*. See www.schooner race.org for full details. Do not miss the Parade of Sail event.

The Canton waterfront (22), the final stretch of the waterfront promenade, runs from Chester Cove about 1 mile east to Canton Waterfront Park. Along the way you pass the

The Canton Marina at sunset

Anchorage Marina and Baltimore Marine Centers, which offer numerous views of sailboats, yachts, and their reflections. This is a photo-rich place when fog sets in. Predawn and first light scenes of the industrial skyline and port activity across the river evoke memories of what the Inner Harbor area looked like early in the 20th century.

On the Dockside Circle waterfront (pedes-trian access near the intersection of Boston Street and South Lakewood Avenue), there is an excellent view of the Baltimore skyline rising above the marina. Sailboats and reflections fill the foreground. Check out the sunset and evening twilight options.

From Canton Waterfront Park, you have an unobstructed view of Fort McHenry across the river, boat traffic along the river, and port activity. Use telephoto lenses up to 400mm to good advantage here.

During the late afternoon and evening twilight, make your way around landmark **O'Donnell Square (23)** in historic Canton. The four short blocks between South Elwood and South Linwood avenues are crammed full of incredible murals, tavern and pub signs, historic row houses, and illuminated restaurants. Shoot twilight streetscapes, candid photos of colorful characters, nightlife locales, and architectural details.

Starting in the 1930s, **Natty Boh (24)** and his handlebar mustache served as the advertising logo for National Bohemian Beer. Now mustachioed Natty Boh is another favorite *eye*-con of Baltimore. He stands high atop Brewers Hill and keeps watch over Canton, the surrounding neighborhoods, and the harbor. Make your way around Brewers Hill to photograph the many and varied places he appears: tavern windows, light sconces, building murals, and so on. My favorite image is an evening twilight streetscape of Natty Boh Tower. From South Conkling Street proceed several hundred yards east along O'Donnell Street, then turn and look back. The large neon Natty Boh sign atop the building glows red against the evening twilight sky, while the traffic flows past at street level.

Directions: From Chester Cove drive 1.8 miles east on Boston Street. Turn left on South Conkling Street. Proceed 3 blocks to O'Don-

Natty Boh, a Baltimore eye-con

Defenders Day at Fort McHenry

nell Street atop Brewers Hill. On-street parking is generally available. Walk 0.3 mile west (downhill) along O'Donnell Street to historic O'Donnell Square.

Sites and Events outside the Inner Harbor

During the War of 1812, **Fort McHenry (25)** defended Baltimore from an attack by the British. As every schoolchild knows, this bombardment inspired Francis Scott Key to write "The Star-Spangled Banner," a poem that later became the national anthem of the United States.

Fort McHenry is open year-round, and a visit to this historic National Park Service site is highly recommended. Tour the bastions, ramparts, and dry moat. One of the best times to visit and photograph is during the annual Star-Spangled Banner Weekend in early September, when Fort McHenry commemorates Defenders Day with military reenactors, musket and cannon firings, a parade, and Saturday evening fireworks. In September 2012, Fort McHenry will host a series of special events during the War of 1812 Bicentennial Celebration. See www.nps.gov/fomc for full details.

The Seawall Trail affords excellent views of the port activity directly across the river. Late afternoon, with the sun behind you, is ideal for photos of the large container ships and the gigantic dockside cranes, as well as other boat traffic on the water. During the winter months, photograph a variety of migratory waterfowl from along the Seawall Trail. Foggy conditions create an ethereal atmosphere.

Traditional brick and Formstone row houses in Federal Hill

Directions: From I-95 North take Exit 55. Drive 0.5 mile and bear left at the traffic light onto Key Highway. Proceed 0.5 mile to Lawrence Street and turn left. At the next intersection, turn left on East Fort Avenue and drive 1 mile to the Fort McHenry entrance.

The **Federal Hill (26)** neighborhood lies due south of the Inner Harbor. It traces its history to the early 1600s, when Captain John Smith described it during his voyage of discovery up the Chesapeake Bay. Navigate your way to the Cross Street Market. During the day, have fun photographing the butchers, fishmongers, flower stands, and fresh produce stalls. During evening twilight, capture streetscapes featuring the colorful murals and signs outside the area pubs. The neighborhood is full of town houses and buildings that date from the 18th, 19th, and early 20th centuries, so there are plenty of architectural styles and details for you to capture, including the locally famous marble front stoops and Formstone facades. Look for painted screens, a folk art tradition that originated in Baltimore's ethnic neighborhoods. Federal Hill has a number of interesting views of Domino Sugar from along Key Highway, Gittings Street, and Clement Street.

The oft-repeated Monty Python phrase "and now for something completely different" aptly describes the **American Visionary Art Museum (27)**, located at the corner of Key Highway and Covington Street. The giant whirligig and exterior mosaic provide the photographer an array of abstract shapes, patterns, and colors to shoot. The museum's neon signs are popular evening twilight subjects. Each May the museum sponsors the Kinetic Sculp-

A feline participant in the annual Kinetic Sculpture Race

ture Race. Where else can you photograph human-sized bees pedaling beehive bicycles, or ancient Egyptian pharaohs rowing a papyrus boat across the harbor (*ankh*-ers away)?

Formerly a Procter & Gamble soap manufacturing facility, **Tide Point (28)** is now an office park located on the waterfront in the historic Locust Point neighborhood. The various buildings provide ample architectural details. Photograph old anchors and ship propellers scattered about the grounds. Expansive water views are the main attraction here. Early morning and late afternoon provide the best light for capturing the boat traffic streaming in and out of the Inner Harbor, in particular visiting tall ships and the USS *Constellation* turn-around voyage. Here, too, you have excellent opportunities to photograph off-loading operations at Domino Sugar: container ships, gigantic industrial cranes, conveyor belts, smokestacks, and more.

Parking on-site is by permit only, but parking is generally available on surrounding neighborhood streets.

Directions: Take East Fort Avenue to Hull Street. Turn left. Tide Point is 0.5 mile ahead on the left.

When built in the early 1900s, the **Bromo Seltzer Tower (29)** was Baltimore's tallest

Tide Point is a former Procter & Gamble soap factory.

building. Today it provides studio space for visual artists. Modeled after the Palazzo Vecchio in Florence, it provides a number of interesting architectural details to shoot, in particular the clock faces. Evening twilight streetscapes featuring this historic building help round out your visual story of downtown Baltimore. The tower is located three blocks west of the Inner Harbor at Lombard and South Eutaw streets.

We in Baltimore know that *hon* is a term of endearment, short for *honey*. Use of the word *hon* is widespread throughout the Baltimore neighborhoods of Dundalk, Essex, Hampden, and Highlandtown. The word is a way of being civil and polite, yet informal all at once. In essence, the use of *hon* is a way to draw closer to those you meet. For more than 15 years, tens of thousands of visitors from throughout Baltimore, the Mid-Atlantic region, and a host of foreign countries have flocked to Hampden each year in early June for **Honfest (30)**. It is a hilarious weekend-long experience. Beehive hairdos, blue eye shadow, housedresses, and spandex fill four city blocks. Pink flamingos and leopard-print-clad women weave their way through the crowd. The fragrance of Aqua Net hairspray wafts through the air, as does the delicious aroma of funnel cakes, crabcakes, hot dogs, brats, kettle corn, and raspberry lemonade (getting hungry?). The crowning event is the Best Hon Contest. Contestants undergo a rigorous (make that sidesplittingly funny) evaluation of their Bawlmerese elocution, talent, and costumes. See www.honfest.net for full details.

Directions: From downtown Baltimore take I-83 North to Exit 8, Falls Road. Continue north along Falls Road to West 36th Street (known in Hampden as The Avenue). Follow the signs to Honfest parking.

In December return to Hampden to photograph the **Miracle on 34th Street (31)**. Lots of

Baltimore's landmark Bromo Seltzer Tower provides creative space for artists.

trumpet-tooting angels, ice-skating snowmen, and nose-glowing reindeer line the street. It is so bright and colorful, astronomers on Alpha Centauri must think they have discovered a new star. It is best to arrive early (parking is generally available on 36th Street . . . where you attended Honfest in June), so you can scout around for your compositions before sunset.

Christmas lights ablaze along 34th Street in Hampden

Wait for evening twilight and be sure to include the sky in your images. That way the holiday lights will stand out against the royal blue sky. In postprocessing, you can change your white balance setting to tungsten for an even stronger contrast. After the sun sets, start shooting and shoot frequently. Check your display until you see that the Christmas lights and the light of the sky provide a good blend and balance. Work fast because you have only about 10 minutes before you lose this balance. Be sure to use a sturdy tripod and a cable/remote release, as exposures are up to one second in length. Again, shoot often and weed judiciously later.

Directions: From downtown Baltimore take I-83 North to Exit 8, Falls Road. Continue north along Falls Road to West 36th Street. Turn right and drive 5 short blocks to Chestnut Avenue. Turn right and drive 4 short blocks to 34th Street.

Another reason to visit and photograph Baltimore in early December is the annual **A Monumental Occasion (32)**. Historic Mount Vernon Place celebrates the holiday season by lighting the Washington Monument. Once the fireworks begin, it is difficult to capture the entire scene. There is little time between bursts, so it's tough to avoid overexposing a wide-angle composition. Try a few full-action images, then use your telephoto lens to concentrate on capturing images that silhouette the statue of George Washington atop the monument against the fireworks bursting in air. Good views abound, in particular near the intersection of North Charles and Centre streets.

On July Fourth and again on New Year's Eve, Baltimore puts on a spectacular **fireworks (33)** show. You have your choice of top-notch views of the Inner Harbor fireworks along the Waterfront Promenade, clockwise from the Rusty Scupper restaurant all the way to Pier 5. Generally, fireworks images work best when a strong compositional element identifies the location; otherwise the images are too generic in appearance. Use the city skyline, the National Aquarium, the iconic Domino Sugar sign, and the reflections across the Inner Harbor waters in your images. With such strong compositions, your viewers will readily see that you captured the moment in Baltimore.

Fireworks light up the Washington Monument in historic Mount Vernon Place.

Crowds are large on July Fourth, so arrive early to stake out your shooting location. Take note of the wind conditions, and position yourself upwind of the smoke the fireworks produce. Use a tripod and cable/remote release. Select the manual shooting mode, an ISO of 200, and an aperture of f/11 or f/16 (for sharp definition of the bright streaks). Set your shutter speed to bulb, and dial in minus 2/3 exposure compensation. The trick is to hold your shutter open for one or two bursts. Multiple bursts often overwhelm the exposure. Crowds are much thinner on New Year's Eve, so you need not stake out and guard a spot hours ahead of the fireworks show.

The historic Patterson Park pagoda aglow on a colorful October evening

Nature in and around Baltimore

We have covered the photogenic cityscapes Baltimore has to offer. Now let's turn our attention to the best nature and outdoor photo opportunities within an easy drive of the Inner Harbor.

Historic **Patterson Park (34)**, known as Baltimore's Best Backyard, is a 150-plus-acre urban oasis that can keep an outdoor photographer busy year-round. More than a hundred species of birds visit the area, including the elusive Baltimore oriole and colorful wood ducks. During the winter and spring migrations, visit the park after a storm. Often high winds offshore blow in an unusual species, such as the recently sighted black-bellied whistling ducks. From late spring through September, visit the butterfly habitat garden, which attracts many of Maryland's native butterflies and nectaring moths. Use other insects found in the various gardens to practice your macrophotography skills. The deciduous trees provide ample intimate fall foliage landscapes. Snow turns the park grounds into a winter wonderland. The historic pagoda looks tremendous in evening twilight and after a winter storm. On the last Saturday before Halloween, photograph the Great Halloween Lantern Parade through Patterson Park. Thousands of children and all those young at heart dress in exceptional costumes. They carry colorful homemade lanterns in a parade that snakes its way up Pagoda Hill. The park is open dawn to dusk.

Sherwood Gardens—Baltimore's preeminent tulip garden

Directions: Head east on Lombard Street. Turn right on President Street, then left on Eastern Avenue. Proceed 1.8 miles to the park on the left.

If you cannot make it to the Netherlands' Keukenhof gardens in the spring, then visit **Sherwood Gardens (35)**, Baltimore's famous tulip garden. Operated by the Guilford Association, the tulips number in the tens of thousands and make a stunning display. The opportunities for flower, garden, insect, and macrophotography are innumerable. The ideal time to visit is mid- to late April. Return in midsummer to photograph bed upon bed of annuals.

Directions: From the Inner Harbor drive 4.4 miles north on Charles Street. Turn right on East Highfield Road. Proceed 3 blocks and turn left on Underwood Road. The gardens are on the left.

The **Howard Peters Rawlings Conservatory and Botanic Gardens of Baltimore (36)**, known unofficially as the Druid Hill Conservatory, is an excellent site for flower, garden, and macrophotography opportunities. The orchid room and palm house are in the original Victorian-era greenhouse, where tripods are welcome. Desert and tropical plants occupy the modern greenhouses. Photograph colorful daffodils and tulips during the spring flower

A pattern of raindrops on a palm leaf at the Druid Hill Conservatory

Ten minutes north of the Inner Harbor is Baltimore's largest garden, **Cylburn Arboretum (37)**, where you can hike more than 2 miles of trails. The Circle, Witch Hazel, and Woodland trails are productive sites for spring wildflowers. In summer bring your macro-photo gear to photograph the rose and butterfly gardens. There are also ample insects, spiders, chipmunks, and mushrooms to photograph. The forest contains oak, beech, poplar, buckeye, and walnut trees, some more than 150 years old. Autumn provides colorful tree canopies and intimate forest scenes, such as acorn and oak leaf groupings on the forest floor. The beautiful old maples supply spectacular color and intimate autumn landscapes. See www.cylburnassociation.org for full details.

Directions: From Baltimore take I-83 North to the Northern Parkway West exit. At the first traffic light, turn left on Greenspring Avenue. Continue through the intersection with Cylburn Avenue, then take the immediate left into the arboretum.

You will find yourself drawn to **North Point State Park (38)** repeatedly throughout the year. It occupies some 1,300 waterfront acres along the Chesapeake Bay. While less than one-tenth the size of other state parks, North Point packs a photographic wallop. Trails lead through woodlands, wetlands, and marshes along the Bay shoreline. Birds are everywhere in these varied habitats. Herons, egrets, and other wading birds spend the spring and summer months in the marsh. Buffleheads, canvasbacks, goldeneyes, mallards, mergansers, ruddy ducks, scaups, swans, teals, and other waterfowl spend November through February in the marsh. Various raptors, small mammals, reptiles, amphibians, songbirds, and spring peepers round out the list of wildlife you may encounter. From late spring through summer, use bug repellent. Poplar and oak dominate the

show. See www.baltimoreconservatory.org for full details about this and other seasonal flower shows.

Directions: From Baltimore take I-83 North to Exit 7 West, Druid Park Lake Drive. At Gwynns Falls Parkway turn into Druid Hill Park. Turn right immediately after entering the park. The conservatory is on the left.

woods, so fall foliage shots are limited in color. While hiking trails are impassable under heavy snow, winter lends an ethereal beauty to the shoreline near parking lot B. Snowcapped boulders reflecting across blue water, ripples frozen in the icy surface of the Bay, a lone bare tree silhouetted against the pastel winter sky, and other winter wonderland compositions are readily available. Sunrise photo ops are precluded because the park opens at 8 AM. Sunset photos are generic in appearance as there is no identifiable foreground or background. See www.dnr.state.md.us/publiclands/central/northpoint.asp for full details.

Directions: From Baltimore take I-695 North over the Key Bridge to Exit 43, Bethlehem Boulevard/Sparrows Point. Turn left on Bethlehem Boulevard. After a little more than 1 mile, cross North Point Boulevard onto MD 20, North Point Road. Proceed 1.9 miles to the park entrance on the left. There is a $3 entrance fee.

The tidal creeks around **Marshy Point Nature Center (39)** form extensive marshlands and wetlands. During the spring and summer months, bald eagles, great blue herons, and ospreys hunt and fish here. Muskrats, otters, and raccoons live in the wetlands but are fairly elu-

Winter calm at North Point State Park

sive. In the winter months, before the waters freeze over and force them far from shore, look for tundra swans and other waterfowl. The trail that leads to an abandoned fishing cabin provides the best view. The center is open daily 9–5, year-round. Hiking trails are open 8 AM to sunset from late spring through fall. See www.marshypoint.org for full details.

Directions: From Baltimore take I-95 North to Exit 67A, White Marsh Boulevard (MD 43). Continue east on MD 43 for 4.7 miles to Eastern Avenue. Turn left and proceed 2.5 miles. Turn right on Marshy Point Road and proceed to the parking lot.

Encompassing nearly 18,000 acres, **Gunpowder Falls State Park (40)** is Maryland's largest state park. The trails wind their way through hilly forests and along the boulder-strewn river in the Hereford and Central areas. Trout fishermen and photographers find the stretch of river between Prettyboy Dam and the Masemore Road trailhead in the Hereford Area particularly productive. Cascade and stream images look best when the rocks and boulders are wet, so visit after a rain or during a light drizzle. That reminds me—sturdy hiking boots are a must. My favorite route in the Central Area is the loop formed by the Wildlands, Stocksdale, and Sweathouse trails. Tulip

Great blue herons live year-round at Marshy Point Nature Center.

Lichen at Gunpowder Falls State Park

A yellow lady's slipper at Oregon Ridge Park

abound: barred owls, chickadees, great blue herons, hawks, kingfishers, turkey vultures, warblers, various woodpeckers, and more. Given the number of gnawed trees along the river, beavers are prevalent. However, I have seen only snakes, turtles, and white-tailed deer. Bug repellent is recommended in the summer months. Yellow and brown hues dominate the autumn scene. To round out your fall foliage portfolio, shoot the broad fall landscapes, then carefully look for forest floor scenics, dappled sunlight coming through the colorful forest canopy, and leaves swirling in streamside eddies. Fine after the first light dustings of snow, the trails in the Hereford Area become dangerously slippery once ice covers them. The park is open dawn to dusk. See www.dnr.state.md .us/publiclands/central/gunpowder.asp for full details.

Note: Copperheads are prevalent in the Hereford Area.

Directions: The Hereford Area is only 45 minutes north of Baltimore. Take I-83 North to Exit 27, Mt. Carmel Road. Turn left on Mt. Carmel Road and drive 0.6 mile to Masemore Road. Turn right and proceed 1.3 miles to trailhead parking on the right.

Directions: The Sweathouse Branch Wildlands Area in the Central Area is just minutes north of Baltimore. Trailhead parking is next to the US 1 bridge over the Big Gunpowder River, north of Perry Hall.

poplar, oak, hickory, and hemlock are the dominant tree species in both areas, so you can capture excellent shots of a typical eastern forest. Skunk cabbage, bloodroot, Dutchman's breeches, toothwort, trillium, trout lily, wild ginger, and wood anemone are among the early spring wildflowers you are likely to encounter. Late spring wildflowers include showy orchis, trailing arbutus, and pink lady's slipper. Birds

Nestled in the hills of northern Baltimore County is **Oregon Ridge Park (41)**. Several miles of hiking trails provide access to excellent spring wildflowers and fall foliage. Pay particular attention to the streamside trail when searching for spring wildflowers. Be sure to photograph the various amphibians and reptiles in the nature center exhibits. During the annual Preakness season, colorful hot-air balloons often launch from this park. See www .oregonridge.org for a trail map and other details.

Directions: Located about 21 miles north of Baltimore. Take I-83 North to Exit 20B, Shawan Road West. Turn left at Beaver Dam Road. Follow the signs to the nature center parking lot.

About 30 minutes northwest of Baltimore is the little gem called **Irvine Nature Center (42)**. Hiking trails meander through forest, meadow, and wetland habitats. Wildlife blinds permit you to photograph various native and migratory birds. Spring wildflowers and intimate fall foliage scenes abound, especially at the forest edge. Visit the outdoor aviary and the critter exhibits inside the nature center, where you have the opportunity to capture images of several raptors, an opossum, and various snakes, turtles, and terrapins under controlled conditions. All this in just 116 acres. Open daily 9–5. See www.explorenature.org for full details.

Directions: Located in the Owings Mills area, about 20 miles northwest of Baltimore. Take I-695 West to Exit 19, I-795 toward Owings Mills. Take Exit 4 and follow the signs for Owings Mills Boulevard. After 2.6 miles turn right at Crondall Lane. Turn right at Garrison Forest Road and drive 0.2 mile to the entrance on the left.

Long before Europeans settled North America, serpentine grasslands covered much of what is now Baltimore and extended north into

A playful opossum at Irvine Nature Center

*Play peeka*hoo *with raptors at Soldiers Delight Natural Environment Area.*

Pennsylvania. Today serpentine grasslands cover less than a thousand acres in Maryland, and more than 90 percent of this once wide-spread habitat lies within **Soldiers Delight Natural Environment Area (43)**. Soldiers Delight features one of the rarest natural ecosystems in Maryland, and work is under way to recover more of it. The harsh soil and weather conditions at Soldiers Delight support a large number of rare plants, minerals, and insects. Spring and fall are the best times for landscape and nature photographers to explore the 7 miles of hiking trails that loop through the area. The aviary at Soldiers Delight cares for rehabilitated but nonreleasable raptors. Two or more times each year, the Feathers in Focus program affords an opportunity to photograph bald eagles, golden eagles, various hawks, American kestrels, and adorable eastern screech owls. See www.dnr.state .us/publiclands/central/soldiersdelight.asp for full details.

Directions: Located in the Owings Mills area, about 25 minutes northwest of Baltimore. Take I-695 West to Exit 19, I-795 toward Owings Mills. Proceed to Exit 7B, Franklin Boulevard West. Turn right on Church Road, left on Berryman Lane, and left on Deer Park Road. The trailhead overlook is 0.5 mile on the right, and the visitors center is another 0.5 mile down the road on the right.

One of the oldest, largest, and finest of Maryland's parks, **Patapsco Valley State Park (44)**, follows the river valley for some 30 miles through three counties. Each of its eight separate areas is an easy commute from Baltimore. The park teems with amphibian, bug, spider, bird, mammal, fall foliage, forest, river and stream, and wildflower photo ops. If you exhaust all those possibilities, point your camera at the ruins of an old flour mill, the historic Thomas Viaduct, fly fishermen casting for

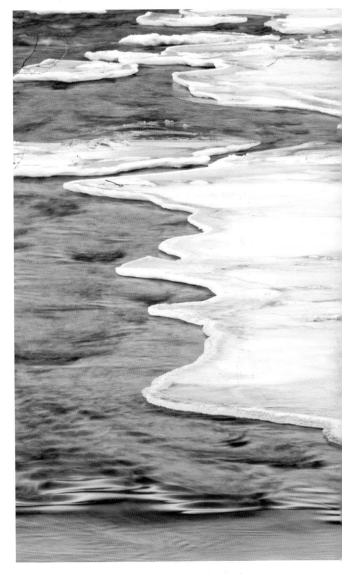

An icy landscape at Patapsco Valley State Park

trout, or mountain bikers descending steep trails. Landscape and nature photographers develop sore shutter fingers.

Directly across the swinging bridge in the Orange Grove Area, the Cascade Falls Trail ascends through a hardwood forest and leads past gigantic boulders to a gentle 15-foot waterfall. The trail continues upstream. Careful—the

The large, round, purple eyespots of the buckeye butterfly are unmistakable.

rock ledge directly above the waterfall is slippery and dangerous. On the Sawmill Branch Trail, boulder-hop your way along babbling brooks, S-curves in the stream, and rocky cascades. Combine this trail with the riverside Grist Mill Trail (through the old tunnel under the railroad tracks) and the Buzzards Rock Trail for a moderately strenuous and scenic loop. You may see red foxes, white-tailed deer, raccoons, great blue herons, wood ducks, and barred and great horned owls along this loop.

At the McKeldin Area in Carroll County, follow the riverside Switchback Trail to the cascading rapids, which are particularly scenic after a rain, in fog, and during autumn and winter. Snakes, especially the northern water snake, like to sun themselves on the exposed rocks near the rapids, so you can capture great habitat images with your telephoto lens.

Open daily 9 AM to sunset, year-round. See www.dnr.state.md.us/publiclands/central/patapsco.asp for full details and driving directions to each area.

Brookside Gardens (45) covers some 50 acres in Wheaton. Photograph small frogs sitting on lily pads in the aquatic garden, dew-covered bumblebees and insects waiting for the sun's warming rays, exquisite floral patterns and shapes in the rose garden, and more. Of particular note is the annual Wings of Fancy live butterfly exhibit. Most weekends from late May through early September, photographers are allowed entry to the exhibit two hours ahead of the general public. Here is your chance to photograph butterflies from North America, Central America, and Asia in natural settings. Endangered species such as the Baltimore checkerspot are included. Tripods are welcome. These photo sessions are wildly popular, so register early. Open sunrise to sunset. See www.montgomeryparks.org/brookside for full details.

Directions: From Baltimore take I-95 South to Exit 33, MD 198 West. In approx. 10 miles, turn left on MD 650, New Hampshire Avenue. Proceed 3.5 miles and turn right on Randolph Avenue. Drive 1.7 miles to Kemp Mill Road, turn left, and continue 0.4 mile to Glenallan Avenue. Turn right and proceed 0.5 mile to Brookside Gardens on the left.

A little over one hour from Baltimore is the photo-rich **Lilypons Water Gardens (46)**,

where photographers are graciously allowed to roam around the 300-acre site during normal business hours. Capture images of delicate water lilies and lotuses reflected in the water, tiny frogs on lily pads, dragonflies on thin plant stalks, and red-winged blackbirds on cattails, to name but a few photo ops. Open daily 9–6, March through June; 10–5, July through October. See www.lilypons.com for full details.

Directions: From I-270 take Exit 26 and follow MD 80 West for 1.5 miles. Turn left on Park Mills Road, continue for 3.5 miles, and turn right on Lily Pons Road. The entrance is about a mile along on the right.

Water lilies abound at Lilypons Water Gardens.

The City Dock area in historic Annapolis is known locally as Ego Alley.

II. Annapolis and Points South

Annapolis

Annapolis is a city steeped in history. George Washington and other Founding Fathers visited and worked here. The city even served as our nation's capital for a short time. While other colonial towns may claim to have finer 17th- and 18th-century buildings than Annapolis, there is no *mast* confusion regarding its claim as the Sailing Capital of the World. Sailing has always been fundamental to the life and economy of the city. That's one reason the United States Naval Academy has been here for more than 160 years. Use your sextant and nautical charts to plot a course to Annapolis, where you will find a number of photo opportunities among the Colonial buildings and along the narrow cobblestone streets.

Directions: Annapolis is a 40-minute drive from Baltimore. Take I-97 South to US 50 East. Take Exit 24, Rowe Boulevard, to reach the historic district. Parking is generally plentiful, and fees are a bargain compared to those in Baltimore.

Navigating your way around Annapolis is simple because it is a town designed for walking. Church Circle and State Circle occupy the high points, and City Dock lies downhill on the water. From these three sites, streets branch out like the spokes of a wheel. My description of what to shoot starts at City Dock, but you can start your photo tour at any of the three main sites.

As it has for hundreds of years, **City Dock (47)** serves as the city's center of activity. Boat watching is a favorite pastime, as boaters parade everything from dinghies to mini-*QE2*s with equal pride, so locals affectionately call

Navy midshipmen crossing Spa Creek Bridge

the dock Ego Alley. Predawn, early morning, late afternoon, and evening twilight each offer excellent photo opportunities. Use a wide-angle lens and a graduated neutral-density (grad ND) filter to capture images of City Dock

The Maryland State House is the only U.S. state house to have served as the nation's capitol.

here. It and other historic boats evoke the beauty, charm, and authenticity of yesteryear. The sleek lines and bright white hulls of modern powerboats stand in strong contrast to the blue water and provide dazzling reflections.

Once you have captured first light at City Dock, make your way uphill to the **Maryland State House (48)**. Its wooden dome is a beloved icon of both Annapolis and Maryland, so much so that it appears on Maryland's commemorative state quarter. It has the distinction of being the oldest state capitol in continuous legislative use in the United States. Proceed around State Circle to capture images of the majestic white dome rising through the trees. Silhouette the statues of famous figures from Maryland history against the dome. Early morning, late afternoon, and early evening light provide excellent illumination.

Thanks to the historic buildings, many cobblestone streets, and angled intersections, there are a number of scenic **streetscapes (49)** between City Dock and State Circle. Early morning to midmorning, check out these three views.

• Francis Street branches off from Main Street and proceeds diagonally uphill toward State Circle. The state house dome peers down from the end of Francis Street, while the iconic St. Anne's steeple rises above the shops lining Main Street.

• The charming and slightly crooked Capital Teas shop sits on the corner of Cornhill and Fleet streets. The state house stands at the upper end of Cornhill Street. Often the neighboring houses display various flags and banners, which add a unique touch to images captured here.

• From the corner of Prince George Street, look up past the picturesque

with the iconic Annapolis skyline in the background: the Maryland State House to the east and historic St. Anne's Church at the top of Main Street. Use a telephoto lens to capture nautical and architectural details as well as candid people shots, such as midshipmen making their way around the dock.

Pro tip: The look and feel of the images you create at City Dock will depend on what's in port. The *Stanley Norman,* one of the Chesapeake Bay's few remaining skipjacks, is often

shops on Maryland Avenue toward the state house. The dome glimmers in early morning, late afternoon, and evening twilight.

To enhance your images of these street scenes, wait for a pedestrian in bright clothing or some midshipmen to walk into your composition. For best results most days, use a wide-angle lens, polarizing filter, and 1-stop grad ND filter.

In late afternoon, return to the intersection of Main and Francis streets. The sun now illuminates the opposite side of Main Street as well as the other side of the state house. During evening twilight at this intersection, use a low ISO and slow shutter speed to turn the brake lights of passing cars into red streaks of light.

Pro tip: These side streets generally include a variety of overhead wires. Instead of driving yourself crazy trying to eliminate them completely in camera or postprocessing, embrace the wires. Incorporate them as necessary elements in your compositions. Use them as leading lines or to anchor the corners of your shots.

From City Dock make your way south along Compromise Street to the **Spa Creek Bridge (50)**, which connects Annapolis to historic Eastport. The bridge provides an excellent vantage point to capture marinas full of boats gleaming in the early morning light, sailboats shimmering on the water in late afternoon, and spectacular sunsets over the creek and coves. Telephoto and wide-angle photo ops abound.

From your vantage point on the bridge, you can see that Annapolis lies northwest of Eastport across Spa Creek. You may begin to anticipate (salivate even) capturing the Annapolis skyline reflected across the water. Unfortunately, all the good views of Annapolis from Eastport are from members-only marinas, restaurants, or private homes packed along the shoreline. If you know someone with a boat moored here, great, but I recommend that you not trespass on private property. Do check out Eastport's pocket parks, such as Leon Wolfe Park at the end of Fourth Street, for possible compositions of marina activity. Also visit the **Annapolis Maritime Museum (51)** (www.amaritime.org), which features a number of interesting exhibits about the Chesapeake Bay.

A picturesque narrow street in Annapolis

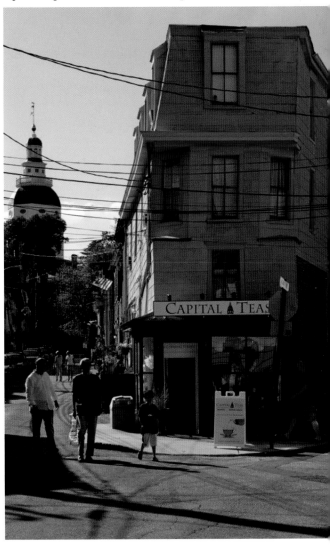

At the museum dock, you may find old fishing boats tied up, as well as local fishermen trying their luck catching crabs. In the summer months, the museum offers three-hour boat trips to the Thomas Point Shoal Lighthouse, a beloved and enduring symbol of the upper Chesapeake Bay. The museum is open noon to 4 PM Thursday through Sunday.

Directions: The Annapolis Maritime Museum is located at 723 Second Street in Eastport.

A visit to Annapolis would be not be complete without a tour of the **United States Naval Academy (52)**. You need a photo ID to enter the academy grounds. You may photograph anything on the grounds except the entry gates and the gate guards. From the seawall along Turner Joy and Sims roads, there are views looking east and south across the Severn River and Spa Creek. In addition to sailboat activity, you may see midshipmen conducting naval exercises along the Severn River in yard patrol craft (oceangoing vessels 80–100+ feet in length). The Main Chapel has spectacular stained-glass windows, several designed by Tiffany. Weekdays during the academic year, catch the noontime formation of the midshipmen at Tecumseh Court. The Armel-Leftwich Visitor Center is open daily 9–5, March through December; 9–4, January and February. See www.navyonline.com for full details.

Directions: From City Dock proceed 2 blocks east along Randall Street to Gate 1, the visitor entrance, and proceed to the Armel-Leftwich Visitor Center.

Thanks to its colonial heritage, Annapolis boasts more than a thousand fine 17th- and

A postcard of the McNasby Oyster Company at the Annapolis Maritime Museum

Maryland's favorite crustacean plays a big part in the story of the Bay.

18th-century buildings. Spend time scouting the narrow streets and shooting their **architectural details (53)**. Photograph windows, doors, and chimneys that exhibit colonial features. Historic markers are color-coded to identify 17th-century, Georgian, Federal, Victorian, and other architectural periods. Also look for the style of brickwork known as all-header bond, which was both difficult and expensive to construct.

Capture **storytelling images (54)** that round out your visual stories of Annapolis. For example, photograph door knockers, coiled rope, flags, and the like, which illustrate the nautical heritage of Annapolis. Shoot the daily recitation of the Pledge of Allegiance at Chick & Ruth's Delly (8:30 AM weekdays and 9:30 AM weekends) to show that Annapolis is an all-American town. Photograph the soda ma-

chines that honor the military to augment your images of the Naval Academy and midshipmen out and about.

Evening twilight is the best time to photograph the sweeping view of the Naval Academy and the Annapolis skyline from the **World War II Memorial (55)** on MD 450. Use ISO 100 and a narrow aperture so the resultant exposure is several seconds long. This way your composition will include colorful streaks of car lights crossing the bridge and traveling along the split halves of MD 450. Like the overhead wires mentioned earlier, embrace the two tall flagpoles at the memorial in your compositions.

Directions: From Gate 1 of the Naval Academy, proceed northwest on King George Street and bear right on Baltimore–Annapolis Boule-

Officially old: These plaques identify and authenticate a building's historic status.

vard. After you cross the bridge, take the first left into the memorial parking lot.

Events in and around Annapolis

Annapolis is passionate about sailing. From late April through early September, capture some of this energy by photographing the **Wednesday night sailboat races (56)**. Well over a hundred sailboats, a veritable flotilla, participate in various classes. The first gun sounds at 6:05 PM. Sailboats race around marks out on the Bay and return along Spa Creek to the finish line at the Annapolis Yacht Club. The view from out on the water gets you up close to the action. Fellow landlubbers can

An evening view of the Naval Academy and Annapolis from the World War II Memorial

Closing on the finish line at the Wednesday night sailboat races

enjoy excellent views from throughout the harbor and from Susan Campbell Park at the end of City Dock. In particular, I recommend the bird's-eye view of the yacht club and finish line from the Spa Creek Bridge. See www.annapolisyc.com for full details.

Each year from late August through mid-October, the **Maryland Renaissance Festival (57)** gives you the opportunity to travel back in time to Revel Grove, an English village plucked out of the Tudor era. Capture wondrous sights of Henry VIII and several of his wives (heads intact) strolling their realm, knights jousting in full armor, jugglers and jesters performing feats of magic, and artisans crafting and hawking their wares. It is immense fun to roam the village photographing the costumed characters and performers. A wide-angle lens in the 28–70mm range is most useful and versatile. Select the aperture priority shooting mode and an aperture of f/5.6. For best results, do not be shy. Ask folks if you may photograph them, and get close. Fill flash often proves useful. See www.rennfest.com for full details.

Directions: The festival is located at the intersection of MD 450 and Crownsville Road, about 8 miles northwest of Annapolis.

On the first Sunday each month from May through September, West Street in Annapolis metamorphoses into a block-long, pedestrian-only artscape called the **First Sunday Arts Festival (58)**. Artists of all sorts, handicrafters, musicians, street performers, and onlookers come together in a celebration of the arts. Capture images of the artists at work. There is also an excellent view of the shops, restaurants, flags, banners, and people along West Street, with the iconic St. Anne's steeple and state house in the background. Work your way along West Street to find the best composition. See www.firstsundayarts.com for full details.

Late each September, you have the chance to watch folks paint the town red . . . plus lots of other colors. **Paint Annapolis (59)** is one of the major Mid-Atlantic region plein air art competitions. From Thursday morning through Saturday evening, see artists paint scenes throughout the historic city. It is a great way to capture unique images of Annapolis as well as spark your own creative juices. Be sure

A colorful court jester entertains one and all at the Maryland Renaissance Festival.

to ask the artist for permission to photograph her or him. See www.paintannapolis.com for full details.

Annapolis celebrates the Fourth of July as well as New Year's Eve with a magnificent **fireworks (60)** show along the waterfront. As mentioned in the Baltimore section, fireworks images look best when you include a strong compositional element that identifies the location; otherwise the images are too generic in appearance. Annapolis launches its fireworks from a barge off the seawall near the Naval Academy. You would have to be on a boat to capture both the skyline and the fireworks, but then you would have difficulty getting a sharp image. Thus, for July Fourth your best vantage point is the Spa Creek Bridge, which has lots of sailboats in the foreground and the Naval Academy in the background. Colorful reflections of the fireworks across the water enhance your images. The ideal vantage spot for New Year's Eve is along City Dock near Pusser's Caribbean Grille. Sailboats strung with sparkling holiday lights are often in the foreground at this dockside location. The fireworks burst over and between the sailboat masts and reflect in the water directly ahead of you. On New Year's Eve, you have two chances to watch the fireworks—during the family-friendly show at 7:30 and again at midnight.

Fireworks light up the sky and reflect across the water of City Dock.

Nature in and around Annapolis

At the west end of Spa Creek sits **Truxtun Park (61)**, the largest park in Annapolis. The boat launch area and the bluff above provide a panoramic view of the many sailboats and yachts moored in the creek, as well as the distant city skyline. From here make good use of both morning and late afternoon light. Capture the changing seasons: In the warm months, plenty of colorful boats fill the foreground. In the winter months, ducks, geese, and gulls waddle about on the icy creek.

Note: In the neighborhoods that border Spa Creek are a number of street-end parks that provide a bit of greenery and a water view. Take a moment to pop into any of these pocket parks. Serendipity may reward you with an unexpected photo op.

Annapolis from Truxtun Park

Directions: Truxtun Park is a 10-minute drive from City Dock. Cross the Spa Creek Bridge into Eastport. Turn right on Chesapeake Avenue. Merge left onto Bay Ridge Avenue. Turn right on Tyler Avenue, which becomes Hilltop Lane after several blocks. Turn right on Primrose Road and follow the signs for the boat launch.

Thomas Point Park (62) sits on a tiny peninsula at the confluence of the South River and Chesapeake Bay. Popular with anglers as well as families on picnics, this park provides photographers a view of the full span of the Chesapeake Bay Bridge (known locally simply as the Bay Bridge) and oceangoing container ships moored on the far side of the channel. Look east-southeast for a view of the Thomas Point Shoal Lighthouse, which has stood steadfast here since 1875. With a telephoto lens in the 400mm+ range you can produce a good shot of this national historic landmark, but the best images are available only from a boat. Last but certainly not least, quite a number and variety of songbirds, wading birds, raptors, and migratory waterfowl are present seasonally. Open daily 8 AM to half an hour before dusk.

Directions: About 6 miles from City Dock. Cross the Spa Creek Bridge into Eastport. Turn right on Chesapeake Avenue. Merge left onto Bay Ridge Avenue, turn left on Bay Ridge Road, and turn right on Arundel on the Bay Road. Follow Thomas Point Road to the end. A parking pass (obtainable at Quiet Waters Park, 600 Quiet Waters Park Road) is required April through October.

A squabble of ring-billed gulls takes flight at Sandy Point State Park.

Families flock to **Sandy Point State Park (63)** in the summer months for boating, crabbing, fishing, hiking, picnicking, and swimming. Photographers find this park along the Chesapeake Bay of interest year-round. There are magnificent views of the Bay, the colorful red Sandy Point Shoal Lighthouse, the towering 4.4-mile-long Bay Bridge, and boat traffic (sailboats, tugs, huge container ships, etc.). By providing essential habitat, the park serves as an important stopover for birds migrating along the Atlantic Flyway. Ducks, geese, gulls, marsh birds, shorebirds, songbirds, wading birds, and woodland birds abound. See www.dnr.state.md.us/publiclands/southern/sandy point.asp for details about entrance fees and operating hours.

Directions: From Annapolis take US 50 East to Exit 32, Sandy Point State Park, the last exit before the Chesapeake Bay Bridge toll plaza.

Jug Bay Wetlands Sanctuary (64) near Annapolis, Monie Bay near Deal Island in southern Maryland, and Otter Point Creek in Harford

marsh boardwalk below the center offers an up-close view of large swaths of aquatic plants. Look for basking turtles and water snakes. At the very least, hike the loop formed by the Otter Point, Railroad Bed, and Two Run trails. Together they afford excellent views of river and wetland scenery, beaver dams and ponds, and a variety of plants and birds. In early to mid-autumn, consider hiking farther to Pindell Point. Here you can frame Canada geese and other migratory waterfowl against the blaze of fall color along the shoreline. Two old barns on the property look spectacular backed by autumn foliage on a blue-sky day.

Research priorities limit public operating hours (9–5 Wednesday and Saturday, year-round; 9–5 Sunday, March through November), but it is a simple matter to time your visits to take advantage of the best light and seasonal conditions. See www.jugbay.org for full details.

Directions: From Annapolis head south on MD 2, Solomons Island Road. At the second traffic circle (approx. 13 miles), exit onto MD 408, Marlboro Road. About 1.4 miles ahead turn left on MD 259, Greenock Road. After 2.7

An eastern red-bellied turtle and a painted turtle catch some sun at Jug Bay.

County comprise the Chesapeake Bay National Estuarine Research Reserve of Maryland. Here scientists study how to better protect wetland environments and enhance the well-being of the Chesapeake Bay.

Jug Bay Wetlands Sanctuary covers more than 1,500 acres of freshwater wetlands, forests, meadows, and fields along the Patuxent River. The sanctuary offers 15 miles of hiking trails, boardwalks, and wildlife observation blinds. The Wetlands Center Observation Deck provides a panoramic view, and the

miles turn left on MD 258, Southern Maryland Boulevard. Continue 1.5 miles to the sanctuary on the left. Follow the gravel road approx. 1 mile to the parking area.

Points South

The Chesapeake Bay is the largest estuary in the United States. With its tidal tributaries, the Bay has a shoreline longer than that of the West Coast. Once you have captured the visual charms, both manmade and natural, that Baltimore and Annapolis have to offer, turn your attention to the photogenic bounty the Bay and Maryland's Eastern Shore provide. As they have for generations, watermen ply the Chesapeake Bay in search of crabs, fish, and oysters. Their workboats and colorful gear fill many a scenic harbor. Historic schooners, maritime museums, and tall ships evoke the glory of bygone days. Tens of thousands of migratory ducks and geese flock to the Bay and its marshy areas. Be on the lookout for bucolic towns, annual festivals, old barns and pastoral landscapes, the endangered Delmarva fox squirrel, natural areas, lighthouses, and ospreys and bald eagles. All this and more awaits you along Maryland's Eastern Shore. You will need several days in each area just to scratch the surface.

As you travel the Eastern Shore, photograph subjects that illustrate the rich history of life on and along the Bay: piles of commercial fishing nets and buoys, stacks of crab pots, old buy boats and skipjacks in a harbor, and whimsical nautical objects such as lighthouse mailboxes and colorful weather vanes.

Start your photo journey by exploring the small towns and country roads that wind their way through Calvert and St. Mary's counties south of Annapolis. Explore all the nooks and crannies the picturesque fishing village of **Solomons (65)** has to offer. Solomons lies at the end of two peninsulas, where the Patuxent River enters the Chesapeake Bay. Surrounded by all this water, you have several brilliant options to capture sunrise. One favorite spot is on Alexander Lane, near the Solomons Yachting Center. Another location, believe it or not, is the small jetty behind the public restrooms on Solomons Island Road. The sailboats, workboats, and yachts provide good foreground elements. Use the reflections of the boats to enhance your compositions. On Farren Avenue near the Chesapeake Biological Laboratory, you have an unobstructed view of the confluence of the Patuxent River and the Bay. Predawn images of container ships out on the horizon are colorful and dramatic. Calvert Marina, located at the end of Dowell Road, can be a good spot for sunrise. Check the evening before to see what is docked here; you need several boats to serve as foreground.

With views across the wide expanse of the Patuxent, you can find good sunset opportunities along the length of the Riverwalk promenade. Look for sailboats or an arrangement of wooden pilings to use as foreground interest in your compositions. Keep an eye on what's happening upriver. You may be lucky to capture an image of the colorful twilight sky above, behind, and reflected below the Governor Thomas Johnson Bridge.

The annual Solomons Plein Air Street Faire in mid-May draws artists from throughout the Mid-Atlantic region and Midwest. Fashion unique images of artists at work throughout the fishing village. See www.solomonsmaryland .com/solomons-paint-the-town-details.html for full details.

Annmarie Sculpture Garden and Arts Center is a 30-acre public sculpture park due north of town. Artsfest in mid-September is a favorite time to visit and photograph. See www.ann mariegarden.org for full details.

Return to Solomons in early December to photograph the annual Christmas Walk, which features a lengthy lighted boat parade.

Golden sunrise over Back Creek on Solomons Island

Directions: From Annapolis travel approx. 30 miles south on MD 2, Solomons Island Road. Turn left on MD 2/MD 4, still Solomons Island Road, and proceed approx. 27 miles to the village of Solomons.

The **Calvert Marine Museum (66)** in Solomons provides a number and variety of photogenic subjects. From its dock, you have a clear view of the Drum Point Lighthouse and its reflection in the water. The dock faces east, so images of the lighthouse are pretty darn good at first light, great in late afternoon (be here on a blue-sky day), and amazing during evening twilight. The museum's collection of historic boats helps you identify the different types of boats Chesapeake watermen use. Mid- to late afternoon provides the best light for boat photos, as well as artistic images of patterns in rotting wood, colorful reflections in the water, and the like. Two river otters live in a large glass enclosure at the museum. Be forewarned—you will shoot plenty of images of this couple. While such images may not grace the cover of a nature magazine, their cuteness rating is high. Along the Marsh Walk at the south end of the dock, herons and egrets often fish in the shallow water. Open daily 10–5. There is an entrance fee. Note that the gate to the marina dock is open even when the museum is closed.

See www.calvertmarinemuseum.com for full details.

Directions: The museum is located at 14200 Solomons Island Road, opposite the visitors center.

The **Cove Point Light Station (67)** is Maryland's oldest lighthouse in continuous operation. The Coast Guard operates the lighthouse, but the Calvert Marine Museum owns it. Although the hours it is open to the public are limited (daily 1–4:30, June, July, and August; weekends and holidays only, May and September), it is well worth a stop as you travel between Solomons and the several nature sites described below. In midafternoon you can capture striking images of the white lighthouse and light keeper's house set against the clear blue summer sky. If present, puffy white clouds enhance your compositions. As we go to pub-

lication, plans are under way to convert the light keeper's house to vacation rental units. When that occurs, renters will be able to take advantage of predawn and evening twilight.

Directions: From Solomons head north on MD 4 3.5 miles and turn right on MD 497, Cove Point Road. The light station is straight ahead another 3.5 miles, at the end of the road.

During prehistoric times, a shallow sea covered much of southern Maryland. When the sea receded, mile upon mile of cliffs became exposed. Wave action over the eons has eroded these cliffs and exposed a variety of fossils, which attract present-day visitors to **Calvert Cliffs State Park (68)**. In addition to prehistoric shark teeth, you can find magnificent first light and early light scenery along the beach. Make sure to explore the forest and creek-side trails. Along the Red Trail (3.8 mile round-trip), cap-

The Drum Point Lighthouse beckons visitors to the Calvert Marine Museum.

The spiral staircase inside the Cove Point Light Station

Out for an early morning walk along the beach at Calvert Cliffs State Park

ture images of the transition from upland forest to tidal marshland to sandy beach. Starting at milepost 1.1, you have excellent views across the marsh formed by beaver activity along Grays Creek. Here you can see numerous reptiles and amphibians (frogs, painted turtles, red-bellied turtles, northern water snakes, etc.) sunning themselves on fallen logs. Herons, ospreys, shorebirds, and songbirds thrive here. Spring and autumn are the ideal times to visit. Fog any time of the year is magical. Obey the signs warning of danger along and below the cliffs. Open sunrise to sunset year-round. See www.dnr.state.md.us/publiclands/southern/calvertcliffs.asp for full details.

Directions: From Solomons drive north approx. 6 miles. Turn right on MD 765 and follow the signs to the park.

Flag Ponds Nature Park (69) is an excellent complement to Calvert Cliffs State Park. Bay views, beachscapes, and cliff scenery look good in early morning and midmorning light. Late spring wildflowers such as columbine and blue flag iris bloom here in May. Longer trails wind through forestland where you often see wild turkeys. Several boardwalks and observation blinds provide access to two freshwater ponds, Duncan's Pond and Richardson's Pond, home to herons, ospreys, a variety of migratory waterfowl, muskrats, river otters, raccoons, and other critters. Open daily 9–6, Memorial Day through Labor Day; weekends only the rest of the year. There is an entrance fee. See www.calvertparks.org for full details.

Directions: From Solomons drive north 7.5 miles on MD 2 Solomons Island Road. Turn right on Flag Ponds Parkway and follow the signs to the parking area.

Parkers Creek is the last remaining undeveloped stream on the Chesapeake Bay's western

A raccoon on a sunken log in a marsh pond

shore. Parts of the creek area look much like they did when Captain John Smith first sailed up the Bay in 1608. With distinct upland forest, wet streamside forest, wetland, and seashore ecosystems, Parkers Creek is an estuary, a mini-version of the Chesapeake Bay. The **American Chestnut Land Trust (70)** protects the creek's watershed area. The north side trails take you along ridge overlooks and through the stream valley. Pay particular attention to the scenery near the intersection of the Double Oak Road Trail and Parkers Creek Trail, as well as that near the Bridge Spur. The south side trails wind past the remains of early homesteads, through hardwood forest and bottomland swamp (where beavers have indeed been busy). Spring and fall are photo-rich times to visit. Bloodroot, Dutchman's breeches, spring beauty, trout lily, and other spring wildflowers flourish along the Horse Swamp Trail. All trails are open year-round from dawn to dusk. See www.acltweb.org for full details.

Directions: To get to the access road to the north side trails from Solomons, drive north approx. 20 miles on MD 2, Solomons Island Road. Turn right on MD 402, Dares Beach Road. Proceed approx. 2 miles and turn right on Double Oak Road. The access road is 1 mile ahead on the right.

To get to the access road to the south side trails from Solomons, drive north approx. 16 miles on MD 2, Solomons Island Road. Turn right on Parkers Creek Road. Cross MD 765 and turn right on Scientists Cliffs Road. Proceed 0.8 mile to the trailhead parking lot on the left.

After the last Ice Age, bald cypress swamps covered a large portion of the Eastern Shore.

Early morning at Parkers Creek

Bald cypress knees frozen in the grip of winter

Today there are a few small cypress swamps in Maryland, the northernmost limit of this tree's natural range. At **Battle Creek Cypress Swamp Sanctuary (71)**, some trees are more than a thousand years old. The county maintains a boardwalk through the primeval swamp. I recommend a visit in spring before the canopy completely grows over. The best lighting conditions are on days with high overcast skies or drizzling rain. Winter is another great time to visit because ice and snow illustrate that the bald cypress is at its northernmost range here. You may see a number of frogs and snakes during late spring and summer.

Directions: From Solomons drive north approx. 18 miles on MD 2, Solomons Island Road. Turn left on MD 506, Sixes Road, and proceed 1.8 miles to Gray's Road. Turn left, and Battle Creek is on the right in 0.25 mile.

Spend several hours at **Historic St. Mary's City (72)**, an outdoor living history museum and archaeological park. Feel transported back in time as you photograph the costumed docents in and around the restored buildings. Capture the vibrant colors of the fields and gardens from spring through fall. On blue-sky days, head directly to the *Dove,* a replica of the square-rigged merchant ship that brought British colonists here in 1634. The ship faces south-southwest, so it casts a nice reflection throughout the day. The *Dove* has a short turn-around voyage each month during tourist season to equalize wear on the hull. Church Point offers the best vantage point for these voyages. October is a great time to visit. While woodland hiking trails provide intimate fall foliage scenes, the key attraction is the annual Grande Militia Muster. Wander through encampments of reenactors and photograph the colonial militia uniforms, historic armaments, and black powder musket firings. Open seasonally, from mid-March through late November. There is a

A 17th-century militiaman in the state house at Historic St. Mary's City

$10 entrance fee. See www.stmaryscity.org for full details.

Directions: From the north end of Solomons proceed across the Governor Thomas Johnson Bridge to MD 235. Turn left and drive 8.9 miles south to Park Hall Road. Turn right and proceed 1.3 miles to MD 5, Point Lookout Road. Turn left and proceed 2.8 miles on MD 5 to Rosecroft Road. Follow the signs to the visitors center.

Early light on fishing vessels docked along Knapps Narrows on Tilghman Island

III. Maryland's Eastern Shore

Middle Eastern Shore

You have explored and captured the scenic points south of Maryland's capital city. Now head back toward Annapolis and cross the Chesapeake Bay Bridge. Kent Island and Talbot County are smack in the center of Maryland's Eastern Shore. The river views; marshlands, and wetlands essential to the Bay's health; the harbors and commercial fishing boats on Tilghman Island; the watermen heading out to fish as they have done for generations; the picturesque harbor, marina, and maritime museum of St. Michaels; the other historic towns and villages, such as Easton and Oxford; the memorable sunrises, sunsets, and more—all are guaranteed to thrill and excite you and enliven your photography.

The Chesapeake Bay Bridge connects Maryland's western and eastern bay shores at Kent Island. At **Terrapin Beach Nature Park (73),**

The handsome diamondback terrapin is a "species of concern" in much of its territory.

you can find various raptors, migratory waterfowl (most numerous from November through February), and other birds along the nature trail that meanders for a little over a mile around a large pond and through a wetland area. Along the beach, enjoy excellent early morning views of the Bay Bridge. When winds blow westerly at 10–20 mph, the huge kites of parasurfers fill the sky with color. Attach your longest lens to capture images of their airborne acrobatics. Open sunrise to sunset.

Directions: From the Bay Bridge take the first exit, Stevensville. Proceed north on MD 18, Romancoke Road, to the Chesapeake Bay Business Park, the first left. Follow the signs to the nature area parking lot.

Tuckahoe State Park and **Adkins Arboretum (74)** are must-see destinations for nature and outdoor photographers. The state park straddles the picturesque Tuckahoe Creek. Several miles of hiking trails meander through woodlands and marshlands where you encounter various habitats and wildlife. The 5-mile loop along the Tuckahoe Valley and Pee Wee's trails is productive year-round: creek and bog scenes, reptiles and amphibians, detailed forest floor shots, insect and spider macrophoto ops, and colorful autumn foliage. On foggy fall

Parasurfers on Kent Island seem to soar above the Bay Bridge.

The common green darner is one of Maryland's largest dragonflies.

mornings, head to Crouse Mill Pond to photograph the vibrant colors reflected in the water. Stick to marked trails and wear blaze orange during the various hunting seasons. Open sunrise to sunset. See www.dnr.state.md.us/public lands/eastern/tuckahoe.asp for full details.

Adkins Arboretum is a nature preserve. Along 4 miles of trails are examples of the lowland and upland forests, meadows, and wooded wetlands native to the Chesapeake Bay. At the visitors center, use your longest lens to photograph the diverse population of birds perched on branches near the feeders. Capture images of painted turtles, sliders, and snapping turtles from the nearby viewing platforms. Butterflies and moths frequent the native garden area. Wildflowers abound, including four native orchids. Because of the scientific study the arboretum conducts, signs identify these

wildflowers. How easy can it get? Open daily 10–4 except Thanksgiving and Christmas. There is a $5 entrance fee. See www.adkins arboretum.org for full details.

Directions: From the Bay Bridge follow US 50 toward Ocean City. Turn left on MD 404, Queen Anne/Shore Highway. Proceed 7 miles to MD 480, Ridgely Road, and turn left. Take an immediate left on Eveland Road. The park office is about 1 mile ahead on the left, and Adkins Arboretum is about 2 miles ahead on the right.

Easton (75) is the ideal base for your photo tour of Talbot County. Visit the historic district, which guidebooks call the Colonial Capital of the Eastern Shore, and shoot the interesting mix of architectural styles found here. Plan to attend the Waterfowl Festival in

A black Lab competes in Easton's DockDogs contest.

early November. This annual event raises funds to conserve and protect wildlife habitats throughout Maryland. Enjoy photographing the wonderfully detailed wooden decoys and the food vendors shucking oysters. Have tremendous fun capturing images of the diving dogs at the DockDogs competition. See www .waterfowlfestival.org for full details.

Directions: Easton is about 28 miles south of the Bay Bridge along US 50.

Ten miles west of Easton is the wonderfully picturesque port town of **St. Michaels (76)**. Situated on the broad Miles River, it is one of the most popular boating destinations on the Chesapeake Bay. Park in the Chesapeake Bay Maritime Museum lot and explore the town on foot. From sunup to sundown, the marinas are a rich source of photo opportunities. The best vantage points are Muskrat Park and the waterfront walkway at the end of Cherry Street. Explore San Domingo Park (West Chew Street) and the adjacent nature trail, which provide early morning and late afternoon views of watermen and their workboats; wetlands; and various herons, turtles, and frogs. Quite a number of the homes and shops date back to the 18th and 19th centuries. Charming streetscapes and attractive architectural details are plentiful: white picket fences burdened by climbing rosebushes, a colorful toy store, an old-fashioned ice cream parlor, and more. During the St. Michaels Art League's annual Paint the Town plein air event in June, capture one-of-a-kind images of artists at work all over town. See www.stmichaelsartleague.org for full details.

Devote plenty of time to photographing the Chesapeake Bay Maritime Museum, which features the Hooper Strait Lighthouse; a fleet of buy boats, skipjacks, and other historic Bay boats; a re-created crab shanty; a boatbuilding shed; and much more. The lighthouse faces east, so it and its reflection in the water, the historic fleet, and the adjacent harbor serve as excellent first light and evening twilight photo subjects. For early morning photography, enter free of charge via the gate next to the admissions building. The exhibits open at 10 AM, at which time I recommend you pay the entrance fee so you may continue to explore and photograph the exhibits spread over the 18-acre campus. See www.cbmm.org for full details.

Directions: Take Bay Street from historic Easton to MD 33 and proceed west about 10 miles to St. Michaels.

The **Tilghman Island (77)** watermen continue their multigeneration way of life, crabbing, fishing, and oystering the Chesapeake Bay waters. Rugged old buy boats, oyster boats, and a historic skipjack bob in the waters of the basin next to the drawbridge and in Dogwood Harbor about half a mile farther south. Position yourself directly north of the drawbridge for excellent first light, early morning, late afternoon, sunset, and evening twilight views of the boats and activity along Knapps Narrows. Watermen return in early afternoon to midafternoon. Ask permission to photograph them as they offload their day's catch. In Dogwood Harbor, capture images of the workboats and their colorful reflections in the water. Practice your event photography skills during Tilghman Island Day in mid-October. Capture the local fun of the workboat race and boat-docking, oyster-shucking, and crab-picking contests.

During August visit the Black Walnut Point Natural Resources Management Area, located at the island's southern tip. Thousands of monarch butterflies lay over here on their mi-

Another day dawns over picturesque St. Michaels.

gration south. Black Walnut Point is open daily 9–5. Park in the waterfront lot outside the gate and explore the point by foot.

Directions: From St. Michaels proceed 12.5 miles west on MD 33 to the Knapps Narrows Bridge, the drawbridge entry to Tilghman Island.

To put it simply, **Oxford (78)** is a picture-postcard village. Spend a full morning here. Arrive early enough to catch both predawn and sunrise in the harbor at the end of Tilghman Street. A small commercial fishing fleet, various sailboats, and a tiny pier provide picturesque foreground. Return to your car and park along Morris Street. Explore the tree-lined streets, other boatyards, and larger commercial fishing pier near the south end of town (you pass it on the way in). Look for boat models in shop windows, colorful sailing flags, and other images with nautical themes. Town Park provides excellent views of the Tred Avon River. For a real hoot, visit the annual Cardboard Boat Race in June. See www.cardboardboatrace.org for full details.

Directions: From historic Easton head south on Washington Street. Turn right on MD 333, Peachblossom Road. Proceed just over 9 miles to Oxford.

Peering this way at an Oxford pier makes for an unusual shot.

The J. M. Clayton Company is the oldest crab-processing plant in the world.

Lower Eastern Shore

Now our photo journey takes us to the extremes. We travel through ever delightful Dorchester County to the southernmost town in Maryland. Here in Crisfield, we board a boat to photograph the way of life in a fishing village on an island on the outermost edge of the horizon. (Believe me, for a midwestern landlubber like me, taking a 45-minute boat ride to the middle of the Bay is extreme.) We visit one of the largest assemblies of schooners and tall ships in the Mid-Atlantic region, as well as a stunningly beautiful national wildlife refuge, where you are most likely to see the endangered Delmarva fox squirrel, the Goliath of squirrels. We top that off with a trip all the way *downy oshun* (as native Baltimoreans say) to Ocean City, Maryland's easternmost city and ultimate beach destination. Pretty extreme, eh?

Cambridge (79) enjoys a maritime history stretching back to the colonial period. Nowadays, sailboats and yachts fill the marina near Long Wharf. Take advantage of early morning and late afternoon light as well as foggy conditions to capture views of the boats and their colorful reflections. Photograph the historic skipjack *Nathan of Dorchester* on one its many daysails along the Choptank River. During the annual Cambridge Schooner Rendezvous in late October, numerous majestic tall ships, in-

Decoys used during duck-hunting season on Taylors Island

cluding the beloved *Pride of Baltimore II* and *Lady Maryland,* sail into port. Long Wharf, its outer jetty, and the edge of Sailwinds Park opposite the wharf offer the best viewpoints. See www.skipjack-nathan.org and www.cambridge schoonerrendezvous.com for full details.

Beautiful historic homes near the wharf, as well as the historic downtown area, offer streetscape and architectural photo ops. For a quintessential image of the Chesapeake Bay, check along Market Street for early morning views of the J. M. Clayton Company, the oldest working crab-processing plant in the world.

The ideal spot to photograph migratory waterfowl is along the seawall at the end of Oakley Street. On calm winter mornings (the birds stay out on the open water when it's windy), black ducks, canvasbacks, greater scaups, wid-

geons, and others come within 10 feet because locals feed them corn.

Other photogenic annual events include the powerboat regatta in late July, the Choptank Heritage Skipjack Race in September, and the uproarious Crabtoberfest, a wonderful mix of dirndls, lederhosen, Maryland seafood, sausage, and sauerkraut. See www.crabtoberfest .com for full details.

Use Cambridge as your base to spend several days photographing Blackwater National Wildlife Refuge, Hoopers Island, and Taylors Island, described below.

Directions: Located about 45 miles south of the Bay Bridge on US 50.

The office of Dorchester County Tourism describes **Taylors Island (80)** as "a classic illustration of Chesapeake Bay tidal marsh habitat." The west end of the Slaughter Creek Bridge on MD 16 provides excellent first light and late afternoon views of this environment. The sun rises behind a loblolly pine forest on the opposite shore and reflects across the water. Use early morning light to capture images of the workboats and fishing gear at the public boat ramp, due west of the bridge, and on Madison Canning House Road, 5 miles east along MD 16. The tidal marshes support abundant wildlife. Proceed south along Smithville Road. Near Beaver Dam Creek and Moneystump Swamp, use your car as a blind to photograph a raptor perched high on a tree snag or wading birds in the shallows.

Directions: From US 50 in Cambridge go south on MD 16, Church Creek Road. Proceed approx. 16 miles to the Slaughter Creek Bridge at Taylors Island.

On **Hoopers Island (81)**, wonderful views of the Bay, Chesapeake watermen at work, picturesque workboats and colorful gear, charming fishing villages, and beautiful sunsets await the photographer. Tyler Cove Public Boat Dock and Marina near the Upper Hooper Island bridge, Back Creek Public Dock and Marina 2.3 miles south of Tyler Cove, and Rippons Harbor 8.1 miles south of Tyler Cove are all excellent locations for first light, early morning, and afternoon photo opportunities. Ask the fishing crews for permission to photograph them as they load gear and bait early in the morning or off-load their catch in the afternoon. Talk to the fishermen; they have great stories about their generations-long way of life on the water.

Walk to the other side of Rippons Harbor along Steamboat Wharf Road to compose a shot of the workboats, their shimmering reflections, and the bright white historic Hoopers Memorial United Methodist Church in the background. Great blue herons, egrets, and other shorebirds forage in the wetland area at the end of Hoopers Island Road. There is little traffic, so stop on the road's edge and use your car as a photo blind. Nearby, at the end of the day, you can use the reeds along the water's edge to compose sunset and evening twilight images.

The Chesapeake watermen: a way of life for many generations

Directions: From US 50 in Cambridge go south on MD 16, Church Creek Road, and proceed approx. 7 miles to MD 335. Turn left and drive 9.6 miles to the intersection with MD 336. Turn right on Hoopers Island Road. From this intersection it is 6.1 miles to the Upper Hooper Island bridge. The road continues approx. 9 miles to the end of Middle Hooper Island.

The **Blackwater National Wildlife Refuge (82)** is a nature photographer's dream. Spring and summer feature great blue herons, egrets, other wading birds, and ospreys in the wetland areas; songbirds, the incredible Delmarva fox squirrel, and sika deer in the forest area; and plenty of reptiles and amphibians. Tens of thousands of Canada geese, snow geese, and migratory ducks visit Blackwater during the late fall (November and December are generally peak months). Winter is well worth a visit thanks to the large breeding population of bald eagles. Year-round, Blackwater presents some of the most spectacular sunrises and sunsets along the Eastern Shore.

Plan to arrive 45–60 minutes ahead of sunrise to capture images of the stunningly colorful predawn sky and its reflection on the marsh. The ideal vantage point is the right-hand pullout before the bridge on MD 335, approximately .75 mile past the intersection with

Predawn light casts a magical glow over Blackwater National Wildlife Refuge.

Bushel baskets of fresh crabs line a dock on Elliott Island.

Key Wallace Drive. If the refuge opens early, a second predawn/sunrise vantage point is at the end of Observation Access Road past the Marsh Edge Trail. The views from the 4-mile-long paved Wildlife Drive face north and south across water and fields, so you can photograph from sunrise through midmorning and again from midafternoon until evening twilight. A moderate telephoto lens in the 200–300mm range will serve you well, but a 400mm+ lens is best for bird portraits.

Note: You often see bald eagles on Wildlife Drive and Maple Dam Road (in particular, near the Reese Todd Public Landing), which runs along the eastern edge of Blackwater.

Directions: From US 50 in Cambridge go south on MD 16, Church Creek Road. After 2.7 miles turn left on Egypt Road. Proceed about 7 miles to Key Wallace Drive. Turn left and enter Wildlife Drive ahead on the right. Pay the entrance fee for Wildlife Drive at the gate.

From Blackwater take the back road through Bucktown, Bestpitch, and Henrys Crossroads. Drive south on Elliott Island Road through the marshes of the **Fishing Bay Wildlife Management Area** to the end of **Elliott Island (83)**. Several pullouts provide intriguing views of the marsh landscape and the raptors, reptiles, shorebirds, and wading birds that live here. Work your way south during early morning

An American white pelican at the Salisbury Zoo

light, then make your way back north during late afternoon light. If you have blue skies and puffy white clouds, you may think you are in Big Sky Country instead of Maryland's Eastern Shore. The tip of Elliott Island features expansive views west across Fishing Bay and south toward Tangier Sound; Chesapeake watermen and sportfishermen out on the water; herons, ospreys, and shorebirds; and several workboats. This is a great spot to capture images of watermen off-loading bushel baskets of fresh Maryland crabs.

Spend several leisurely hours in **Salisbury (84)**. Photograph white pelicans along the Salisbury Zoo's creek. The cute factor of the zoo's prairie dogs is off the charts. For centuries, decoys played a major role in the life of Native Americans, colonists, and hunters around the Chesapeake Bay. The Ward Museum of Wildfowl Art details the evolution of decoys from utilitarian tools to modern works of art. The museum's nature trail meanders through a wetland habitat where you can photograph a variety of ducks, geese, and herons. See www.salisburyzoo.org and www.wardmuseum.org for full details.

Deal Island and the **Deal Island Wildlife Management Area (85)** are a true joy to photograph. Instead of waterfront condo complexes and McMansion developments, you will find several hundred watermen and their families living and working on the island much as they have done for generations. In Wenona, the largest harbor on the island, there are unobstructed views of commercial fishermen and their fleet. Use predawn, sunrise, and first light to good effect here. In late afternoon, the workboats and their reflections glimmer down the length of the harbor, and the nearby crabber shanties take on an attractive glow. Explore the smaller harbors at Champ Wharf and Deal Point for additional images.

In the early 1900s, watermen began using skipjacks to dredge oysters from the Chesapeake Bay. Out of hundreds that once sailed the Bay, only a dozen or two remain seaworthy today. Over Labor Day weekend, numerous magnificent skipjacks gather and compete in the annual Deal Island Skipjack Race.

In spring through fall, the access roads to the Deal Island Wildlife Management Area teem with a wide variety of wildlife: bald eagles, black-necked stilts, black rat snakes, diamondback terrapins, ducks, egrets, geese, herons, ospreys, red foxes, sika deer, water snakes, willets, yellowlegs, and more. Bring your longest lens and use your car as a photo blind.

Directions: From Salisbury proceed south on US 13 approx. 12 miles to Princess Anne. Turn right on MD 363, Deal Island Road, and proceed approx. 18 miles to Wenona. There are two access roads off MD 363 into the Deal Island Wildlife Management Area. The first entry, 9.3 miles from the intersection of US 13, has no official name, but local inhabitants affectionately call it Done Workin Road. The second entry is Riley Roberts Road in Dames Quarter. Both require a left-hand turn off of MD 363, and both are narrow gravel roads.

Watermen head out toward Tangier Sound to begin the day's work.

Crisfield (86), Maryland's southernmost town, is known as the Crab Capital of the World. Photograph watermen and their workboats, crab shanties, and fishing gear, along with the day's catch, at City Dock, around Somers Cove, and in the small boat harbor off Collins Street directly north of town. The seafood packinghouse opposite City Dock looks fantastic in predawn light and serves as a classic illustration of Maryland's Eastern Shore. At day's end, City Dock provides excellent views of sunset and evening twilight over the marshlands on nearby Janes Island. On Labor Day weekend, head to Crisfield for the annual National Hard Crab Derby. Enjoy photographing the crab races, workboat docking contest, crab-picking contest, and more. See www.crisfieldchamber.com for full details.

Directions: From Salisbury travel approx. 17 miles south on MD 13, Ocean Highway. Bear right on MD 413 and drive about 14 miles south to Crisfield.

Smith Island (87) is an archipelago in the heart of the Chesapeake Bay. The villages of Ewell and Rhodes Point are on one island; Tylerton is on another. The Martin National Wildlife Refuge and several tiny uninhabited islands comprise the bulk of Smith Island. The water views are incredible here. Sunset and twilight are phenomenal. The marshland is a haven for egrets, herons, and ibises. Gulls, oystercatchers, black skimmers, various ducks, migratory waterfowl, ospreys, peregrine falcons, and brown pelicans thrive in the marsh grasses, on the mud flats and sandbars, and along the maze of tidal creeks.

For centuries the crab industry has played the principal role in the island's culture and livelihood. Picturesque crab shanties, workboats, and stacks of colorful crab pots line the harbors and piers. The work basin in Ewell provides a bounty of predawn, sunrise, sunset,

Hot steamed crabs on Smith Island

and evening twilight photo ops. Throughout the day, create images of the old general store, many island cats, and piles of colorful floats and other fishing gear. In the early evening, photograph workers picking the day's catch at the Smith Island Crabmeat Co-op in Tylerton. A visit any time of the year is worthwhile, but

A colorful array of pine needles, pinecones, and lichen cover the forest floor.

my favorite time is the softshell crab season between late May and September.

Rent a bicycle or golf cart to make your way around Smith Island. Drive your cart to catch sunrise, then use it as a blind to photograph birds in the marshes along the road. (Pretty darn cool, eh?) Spend several days here, and be sure to hire a local boatman to take you for a trip up the *guts,* or meandering creeks.

Directions: From City Dock in Crisfield catch a passenger ferry for the 45-minute ride to Smith Island.

On your way back north, visit the **Furnace Town Living Heritage Museum** and **Paul Leifer Nature Trail (88)**. At Furnace Town, capture intriguing images of historic costumes, the old brick furnace used to smelt iron, wooden ore carts, and more. The museum lies within the Pocomoke State Forest, along Nassawango Creek. Bird and nature photo opportunities abound in the general area and specifically along the Nature Conservancy's Paul Leifer Nature Trail: marsh, swamp, and wetland habitats of bald cypress and loblolly pine trees; crane-fly orchids, pink lady's slippers, and other wildflowers; colorful lichen-covered tree trunks and branches; amphibians and reptiles; and birds such as flickers, pileated woodpeckers, and prothonotary warblers. See www.furnacetown.com for full details.

Directions: Furnace Town is about 39 miles northeast of Crisfield. Drive approx. 13 miles north on MD 413. Turn right on US 13 and proceed about 8 miles. Bear right on MD 364, Dividing Creek Road, and drive about 7 miles to MD 12, Snow Hill Road. Turn left and continue 2.8 miles to Old Furnace Road. Turn left and proceed 1.2 miles to the museum on the left.

With its seemingly endless white sand beaches and its famous boardwalk, **Ocean City (89)** is

Ocean City's iconic Boardwalk sign at twilight

the prime summer destination for many Marylanders. On peak-season weekends, several hundred thousand visitors flock here. Visit during the summer to capture images of surfers riding the waves, colorful kites filling the sky, and sand sculptures lining the beach. Rise early to silhouette sportfishermen and beachcombers against the colorful predawn sky; to photograph the rising sun and crashing waves; and to capture shorebirds feeding along the surf's edge. At day's end, capture long exposures of the brightly lit amusement rides set against the twilight sky.

Photographing summer fun in Ocean City is a real hoot, but return here throughout the year. Spring and fall provide many of the same photo ops with cooler temperatures, lower humidity, and considerably fewer people. Photogenic seasonal events include the St. Patrick's Day Parade in March, the Sunfest Kite Festival in late September, and Harbor Day at the Docks in October. In winter numerous migratory waterfowl gather and feed along the jetty at the end of town: gulls, terns, loons, brown pelicans, surf scoters, and more.

No matter the time of year, visit the Isle of Wight Nature Park, a salt-marsh island in the middle of Assawoman and Isle of Wight bays. Marsh birds, shorebirds, and migratory water-

Two wild ponies forage along the road at Assateague Island National Seashore.

cluding a great view of the Ocean City skyline across the bay.

Directions: Ocean City is about 150 miles from Baltimore. Cross the Chesapeake Bay Bridge and stay east on US 50 straight into town.

A quick drive from Ocean City is windswept **Assateague Island (90)**, a narrow barrier island that extends more than 30 miles south along the coast. Folks flock to the northern tip to camp, fish, sunbathe, surf, and swim in Assateague State Park (open 9 AM to sunset).

Capture a wide variety of nature and outdoor images along the Assateague Island National Seashore, a natural environment of sandy beaches, salt marshes, coastal woodlands, and bays. Photograph the famous Assateague wild ponies as they roam the island. You may see them by driving slowly along Bayberry Drive, the only paved road on the seashore. Protect the environment and park in designated areas only. Summers on the island are hot and humid. Biting flies, mosquitoes, and ticks number in the gazillions, so use bug repellent. The wild ponies often visit the beaches, where the sea breeze provides some relief from the summer heat and swarms of bugs. The forest and marsh hiking trails are good places to see the ponies in spring, fall, and winter.

Directions: Take US 50, Ocean Gateway, west from Ocean City. Turn left on MD 611, Stephen Decatur Highway, and proceed approx. 8 miles to Assateague Island.

fowl are abundant. Take the MD 90 bridge and turn left at St. Martins Neck Road.

The commercial harbor on the west side of town is a must-see destination. From Golf Course Road, turn left and park along Sunset Avenue. Capture images of large trawlers, Bay workboats, and colorful fishing gear. You will find a good variety of sunrise, early light, and evening twilight photo opportunities here, in-

Upper Bay

You need several weekends spread over several seasons to begin to capture the photographic wealth of Maryland's Upper Bay: historic lighthouses near Bay headwaters, the largest concentration of bald eagles east of the Mississippi, migratory butterflies and tundra swans, scenic farmland, the narrowest town in America, and much more.

We begin our photo tour in Chestertown, about 45 minutes north of the Chesapeake Bay Bridge. We then travel north and west, cross the mighty Susquehanna River, and end our tour near Havre de Grace, 35 minutes northeast of Baltimore.

Stroll along worn brick sidewalks in **Chestertown (91)**, a scenic riverside village. Photograph the architectural details of the sea captains' homes along Water Street and other historic buildings throughout town. Chestertown features a variety of annual photogenic events. On Memorial Day weekend, Revolutionary-era reenactors, fife and drum corps, and historic ships fill the town with riotous fun during the annual Chestertown Tea Party Festival. See www.chestertowntea party.com for full details. In late September, the Waterfront Festival features a colorful cardboard boat regatta. Each October the Sultana Projects' Downrigging Weekend attracts a fleet of majestic tall ships from as far away as Newport Beach, California. See www.sultana projects.org for full details.

The riverside park at the end of High Street provides excellent first light and early morning views of the schooner *Sultana* clearly reflected in the water. With the sun behind you in the late afternoon, capture images of the *Sultana* figure-

Kent County features many photogenic barns and farm buildings.

head and rigging details from along the wharf. Locations from which to see the *Sultana* and other tall ships under full sail include (1) along MD 289 west of town between Radcliffe Road and Collins Avenue, and (2) the small dock at the end of Quaker Neck Landing Road. (Drive about 4 miles west along MD 289, turn left on Quaker Neck Road, and take the next left on Quaker Neck Landing Road. Proceed about 2 miles to the road's end.)

Kent County is renowned for its farms, including quite a number that have been in operation for more than a hundred years. Views of the numerous barns, silos, and colors and patterns in the crop fields vary by season and throughout the day. Drive the quiet country roads and seek out picturesque farm scenes. See www.kentcounty.com/attractions/farmtour /farmtour.php for a self-guided farm tour map.

Morgan Creek, a tributary of the Chester River, makes a gentle S-curve near Riley's Landing. The view is south down the tree-lined creek. If the wind is calm, consider this an early morning destination in the fall. The autumn colors on the trees, their reflections in the water, reeds in the foreground, and Canada geese out on the creek provide an iconic country photo. To get there, drive 4 miles north on MD 289, turn left on Rileys Mill Road, and proceed to the road's end.

Directions: Chestertown is a 45-minute drive from the Chesapeake Bay Bridge. Proceed east on US 301 about 15 miles and turn left on MD 213, Centreville Road. Continue about 18 miles to Chestertown.

Rock Hall (92) is a peaceful fishing village on a small peninsula. Water, commercial fishing,

Day's end at Rock Hall harbor

A wedge of tundra swans near Eastern Neck National Wildlife Refuge

and pleasure boating images are plentiful. Watermen tie up at the Walnut Street pier and Bayside Landing Park. Use early morning and late afternoon light to photograph the watermen at work: getting ready to go out, returning with their catch, cleaning and stacking their crab pots, and painting and repairing their boats. Head to Haven Harbour Marina on Rock Hall Avenue (MD 20) for images of the many sailboats and pleasure boats bathed in midmorning and midafternoon light. Throughout the day, shoot such whimsical nautical subjects as a garden lighthouse, a pelican yard ornament, a fish mailbox, or the giant rockfish on the village water tower. The Bayside Landing Marina provides both a number and a variety of strong compositional elements for sunset and evening twilight images. If there is dramatic cloud action or color over the distant Bay Bridge, shoot the sunset from Ferry Park on Beach Road.

Rock Hall is filled to capacity during the annual rockfish tournament and July Fourth holiday. Enjoy the Pirates and Wenches Fantasy Weekend in August, when saber-wielding buccaneers and landlubbers alike converge on Rock Hall's shores. Great costumes, lots of merriment, and *arr-arr-arr* mayhem flourish. See www.rockhallpirates.com for full details.

Directions: Rock Hall is a 20-minute drive from Chestertown. Take High Street north, turn left on MD 20, and proceed to Rock Hall.

Eastern Neck National Wildlife Refuge (93) is a winter haven for migratory waterfowl. Plan a visit between December and February, because it is a major stopover for tundra swans. Throughout the year, 6 miles of walking trails, boardwalks, and observation blinds enable you to capture pristine images of the array of habitats encountered around the Bay (tidal marshes, wetlands, and woodlands), numerous species of birds, and various amphibians, butterflies, insects, mammals, and reptiles. The wildlife calendar developed by refuge staff (www.fws.gov/northeast/easternneck/wildlife calendar.html) is an excellent resource to help you decide what to photograph when. July is a favorite time because it is the usual peak period for butterflies. Bug repellent is recommended from late spring through fall.

Directions: From MD 20 in Rock Hall turn left on MD 445. The refuge is approx. 6 miles ahead.

Roughly 10 miles north of Chestertown is the **Sassafras Natural Resources Management Area (94)**, located along the scenic Sassafras River and Turner's Creek. Trails lead through rolling farmland, hardwood forest, and marshland. Here you find numerous nature and outdoor photo opportunities. Beavers, deer, foxes, muskrats, shorebirds, songbirds, turkeys, and migratory waterfowl abound in the mix of habitats. During hunting season, wear blaze orange clothing and stick to the trails. A small number of Chesapeake watermen ply the tranquil waters of Turner's Creek. From the dock near the historic granary, you may have a ringside seat

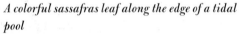

A colorful sassafras leaf along the edge of a tidal pool

Chesapeake watermen working Turner's Creek and the Sassafras River

First light shines on Chesapeake City in Cecil County.

to watch them working their pound nets a hundred yards offshore. In summer American lotus blooms in nearby protected coves. In autumn enjoy brilliant foliage colors surrounding Turner's Creek. Open sunrise to sunset.

Directions: From Chestertown drive approx. 7 miles north on MD 213. Turn left on Kennedyville Road, which becomes Turner's Creek Road at MD 298. Proceed straight 3.5 miles to the trailhead parking. Turner's Creek and the historic granary are at the end of the road, maybe another 0.5 mile beyond the trailhead parking.

Explore **Chesapeake City (95)**, a pleasant village located along the Chesapeake and Delaware Canal in Cecil County. Picturesque Victorian homes and shops date back to the canal's construction in the 1830s. From Charles Street, walk west along the canal to capture predawn images of the Chesapeake City Bridge soaring above its reflection in the water. The grassy area on Second Street near Bethel Road offers remarkable first light and evening twilight views of the bridge towering high above the village and marina. From the pedestrian sidewalk on the bridge, photograph the maritime traffic and the historic village below through breaks between the fencing. There is no established schedule to determine when large container ships pass by. Should you see a red pilot boat head out, a colossal vessel is likely to appear soon.

Directions: Chesapeake City is a 45-minute drive north of Chestertown along MD 213.

Elk Neck State Park (96) sits on a peninsula surrounded by the Chesapeake Bay and its headwaters. Families take advantage of the park's sandy beaches and boat launch facilities. More than 10 miles of trails meander through shoreline, marsh, and forest habitats. The forest supports deer, foxes, and raccoons. In the early winter months, check along the shore for such migratory waterfowl as buffleheads, common goldeneyes, and hooded mergansers. Thanks to its variety of warblers, birders consider the park a prime spring birding location. The Turkey Point Lighthouse sits at the southern tip of the park. You can photograph the lighthouse and its panoramic view of the Bay throughout the day, but first and late light provide the best results.

Directions: From Elkton drive 6 miles west on US 40, Pulaski Highway, to MD 272 South. Continue 11.4 miles south on Turkey Point Road to the state park entrance on the right.

The charming and delightful town of **Havre de Grace (97)** sits alongside the Susquehanna River, the mighty headwaters of the Chesapeake Bay. A 0.75-mile-long waterfront promenade provides panoramic views of the wide expanse of river and Bay. The promenade begins near the Concord Point Lighthouse, the town's well-known landmark. You can photograph the lighthouse to good effect throughout the day and during evening twilight. Farther along, the boardwalk skirts a marshy area that's generally

A red fox checks for danger before proceeding across a snow-covered field.

Concord Point Lighthouse on the autumnal equinox

Four bridges span the Susquehanna River near Havre de Grace.

a productive spot for bird photography. Look here in winter for migratory waterfowl. Next along the promenade is the renowned Havre de Grace Decoy Museum. Discover the fascinating role decoys played in life on and around the Chesapeake Bay and photograph a number of these carved masterpieces. See www.decoy museum.com for full details. The southern terminus of the waterfront promenade is the town marina, home port to the historic skipjack *Martha Lewis* and a few commercial fishing boats.

The colorful signs and display windows of the many galleries, restaurants, and shops provide ample subjects for cityscape images. Several small parks north of the waterfront promenade provide outstanding views of the four bridges spanning the river. Each spring through 2014, reenactors will portray the battle local militiamen fought against British marines during the War of 1812. The annual plein air contest in September can inspire and enhance your composition skills. See www.hdg pleinair.com for full details.

Directions: From Baltimore follow I-95 North about 35 miles to Exit 89. Follow MD 155 another 3 miles into downtown Havre de Grace.

Also situated on the banks of the Susquehanna River is **Port Deposit (98)**, one of Maryland's hidden gems. The river flanks one side of town and towering granite cliffs the other, leaving

After spotting a fish in the river below, a bald eagle dives down to catch it.

space along the shore for only the mile-long Main Street. The local county tourism office refers to it as the narrowest town in America. Beautiful homes and commercial buildings, all built of local granite, line Main Street. Thanks to its rich architectural heritage, you can spend a morning in Port Deposit photographing details of the historic buildings and the colorful, present-day storefronts. In the late afternoon, head to the south end of town to capture images of the four bridges that span the Susquehanna downriver. The entire town is listed on the National Register of Historic Places.

Directions: From Havre de Grace head east across the river on US 40. Turn left on MD 222, Perryville Road, and drive 5.5 miles to Port Deposit. Note that MD 222 changes name from Perryville Road to Bainbridge Road.

Birders and photographers alike consider the hydroelectric **Conowingo Dam (99)** one of the best places east of the Mississippi River to find bald eagles. Anglers, eagles, and photographers alike eagerly await the discharge of fish below the dam. Photography conditions are most favorable. Eagles are present in good numbers throughout the year, you are in close proximity to them, and the sun is behind you. Capture images of bald eagles perched in nearby trees, flying directly overhead, and snatching fish out of the water—or from one another. The eagle population swells from October through March, with the peak period running from late

November through mid-January. Use at least a 300mm lens. A 400mm lens and 1.4x teleconverter are ideal. Bring plenty of memory cards . . . and chemical hand warmers.

All pretty spectacular, eh? But it gets better. Several species of gulls visit in large numbers during the same general period. Downriver a short way, you may see mallards, common mergansers, and other waterfowl.

Directions: From Baltimore travel north on I-95 to Exit 89, Havre de Grace. Turn left on MD 155. Drive 2.2 miles and turn right on MD 161. Proceed 5.2 miles to Stafford Road. Turn right on Shuresville Road. Proceed approx. 1 mile to Shures Landing Road. Turn right and continue to the bottom of the hill. Park in one of the designated spots.

I mentioned in the description of the Jug Bay Wetlands Sanctuary that **Otter Point Creek (100)** is part of the Chesapeake Bay National Estuarine Research Reserve of Maryland. The reserve's scientists study how to better protect wetland environments and enhance the well-being of the Chesapeake Bay. The public may explore several miles of trails through the 400-plus acres of tidal marshes and wooded wetlands at Otter Point Creek. Ducks, shorebirds, reptiles, amphibians, elusive river otters, and wildflowers are some of the fauna and flora you may encounter from early spring through early winter. The Anita C. Leight Estuary Center is the public education facility of the research reserve. At the huge freshwater turtle pond, you can get up close to several species of turtles. The center is open Thursday through Sunday. See www.otterpointcreek.org for full details.

A juvenile northern water snake in Otter Point Creek.

Favorites

Favorite Skyline
Baltimore's Inner Harbor

Favorite Sunrise in Baltimore
Domino Sugar refinery

Favorite Sunrise along the Eastern Shore
Ocean City
Blackwater National Wildlife Refuge

Favorite Watermen Village
Smith Island
Wenona on Deal Island
Hoopers Island

Favorite Streetscape
Pratt Street in Baltimore from the Gay Street
pedestrian overpass

Favorite Commercial Harbors and Marinas
Annapolis
Ocean City
Crisfield
Turner's Creek
Tilghman Island

Favorite Place to Photograph Dogs
Honfest in Hampden
St. Patrick's Day Parades in Baltimore
and Ocean City
Pirates and Wenches Fantasy Weekend
in Rock Hall
DockDogs in Easton

**Favorite Places for Insects, Small Critters,
and Wildflowers**
Patapsco Valley State Park
Flag Ponds Nature Park
Gunpowder Falls State Park
Calvert Cliffs State Park

Shucking oysters fresh from the Chesapeake Bay

Favorite Place for Birds
Blackwater National Wildlife Refuge
Conowingo Dam

Favorite Annual Events
Honfest in Hampden
Crabtoberfest in Cambridge
Privateer Day in Fells Point
Sunfest in Ocean City
Kinetic Sculpture Race in Baltimore
Maryland Renaissance Festival near Annapolis
Fireworks on July Fourth and New Year's Eve
in Baltimore and Annapolis